Foundational Doctrines of the Faith

Knowing what we believe...
...and why

by Elmer L. Towns

Church Growth Institute
Providing Practical Tools for Growth
P.O. Box 4404, Lynchburg, VA 24502

Editor: Cindy G. Spear
Designer: Carolyn R. Phelps
Editorial and Design Assistant: Tamara Johnson

Cover Photography: Les Schofer

Contents

The Holy Spirit guided human authors so that what they wrote in Scripture is accurate and without error. ...Ultimately, the real value of the Bible is realized in our life as we apply the Scriptures to life.

Our view of God will impact the way we live. . . . God is defined as Spirit, a person, life, self-existent, unchanging, unlimited by time and space, and a unity. ...God consistently works out His eternal plan by guiding and overseeing all things by His wise and holy purpose.

Jesus was in fact God incarnate in human form. He is the second person in the Trinity who came to live among us, die for us, and resurrect that someday we might be able to live with Him forever.

The Holy Spirit is not merely a force, but has all the attributes of personality and is also God as the third person of the Trinity. The Holy Spirit's work brings us to Christ and salvation, equips us for ministry, empowers us for service, and produces spiritual fruit in our life.

People are unique beings. Contrary to the evolutionary view of origins, the biblical view of people identifies them as unique from animals, created in the image and likeness of God. People have both a physical and metaphysical aspect – body and soul or spir-

it. Because of our ancestral parent's failure to obey God, sin was introduced into the human experience – causing the need for reconciliation to God our Creator.

The single most significant experience in life is that involved in receiving the salvation provided by Christ on the Cross. This experience involves conversion, regeneration, justification, and sanctification and grants us eternal life with Christ.

Jesus instituted the church as a means of Christians assembling together to encourage and help one another in the Christian life and to enable them to be more effective in reaching out to others. In summary, the "ekklesia" (Greek for church) is a group of "called-out ones" established for worship, instruction, fellowship, and evangelism.

Eschatology literally means "the study of last things." The doctrine of eschatology can be divided into two themes: "personal eschatology" which is the study of God's final judgments and the eternal state – heaven and hell – and "prophetic eschatology" which is the study of the second coming of Christ and the various events related to His return.

Introduction

INTRODUCTION

Many people come to realize their need for a Saviour, repent of their sin, and accept Christ. They are converted and become Christians. They join a church and attend with some regularity. In their zeal and desire to serve Christ and do God's will, some Christians become very active in serving through their church. However, when an outsider, a non-Christian, asks the basis of the Christians' faith, they don't really know how to answer.

A majority of Christians have just enough knowledge and experience to know why a person needs salvation and how to accept Christ as Saviour. They know the Gospel in a nutshell, but have never been taught the *foundational doctrines* of their faith. In order for Christians to remain steadfast and grow stronger in their faith, they need to know what they believe and why they believe it. And to be effective church members who wholeheartedly represent their church, they must learn and support their church's doctrinal beliefs.

This book was written to help new Christians as well as established Christians know and understand basic, foundational doctrines of the Christian faith. Once we learn these basics, we develop stronger roots and are less likely to bend and sway when faced with the winds of false doctrine and wolves who would lead us astray. We can also securely state our position with authority to those who question our faith.

Eight major doctrines are defined and addressed in this book, including what we believe about the Bible, about God, about Christ, about the Holy Spirit, about People, about Salvation, about the Church, and about Eschatology. I encourage you to study them and sink your Christian roots into the fertile soil of God's Word as you seek to follow His will and become a mature Christian.

I recommend that you use the section beginning on page 107 to write down Scripture references and make notes about important points and information you discover in your study. You may also want to jot down specific information from your own church's statement of purpose and doctrinal statement.

May God bless you in your Christian walk.

Elmer Towns

Elmer Towns

Chapter One

CHAPTER ONE

What We Believe about the Bible

No other single book in history has impacted more lives in a positive way than the Bible. Several years ago, a Bible was published which was simply identified as *The Book*. Certainly the Bible is described accurately as the greatest book in the world. It deserves the expression "greatest book" because it is the greatest in subject matter; it is the greatest in influence on lives and nations; and it answers man's greatest need – salvation.

Throughout history, the Bible's significance has been readily recognized by many world leaders. Those who have sought to oppose this book and the faith it teaches have found themselves fighting a losing battle. A Roman Caesar opposed the Bible so vigorously he erected a monument to praise his supposed success in destroying the Scriptures. But when the successor to his throne declared Rome a Christian Empire, more than fifty copies of the Bible came out of hiding and were made public within three hours. For years, Russian Communism attempted to discredit the Bible and Christianity, but today portions of the Scriptures are posted in every schoolroom in the country and Russian leaders are appealing to Christian leaders to help them rebuild their nation.

As Christians, it is important to know what we believe about the Bible and what the Bible teaches concerning other important areas of life. When the Bible refers to itself, it usually does so in the context of one of eight themes. Evangelical Bible teachers have designated certain words rich with meaning to describe these themes. These words include revelation, inspiration, inerrancy, preservation, canonicity, illumination, interpretation, and application. As we understand what these eight words teach us about the Bible, we will come to know what we believe about the Bible.

The Bible: God's Message to Us

The reason we have a Bible at all is because God has chosen to reveal certain truths about Himself to us. The Bible is God's self-revelation of Himself to His people. The word "revelation" refers to the act of God which gave people knowledge about Himself and His creation, including knowledge which they could not have otherwise known. Moses reminded the people of Israel, "the secret things belong unto the Lord our God: but those things which are revealed belong to us and to our children forever, that we may do all the words of this law" (Deut. 29:29).

Our understanding of revelation implies several things. First, revelation is an act of God, "for the prophecy came not in old time by the will of man: but holy men of God spake as they were moved by the Holy Ghost" (2 Peter 1:21). Second, God gives this revelation about Himself to people (1 Cor. 10:6; Rom. 1:19). Third, revelation involves the communication of truth we could not otherwise know apart from God. The apostle Paul described his ability to write Scripture in the context of the Holy Spirit revealing a mystery which was hidden to previous generations (Eph. 3:3-5). Fourth, the revelation which God has given us in Scripture is both partial and complete. It is partial in the sense that God did reveal some things to the apostles which He chose not to include in Scripture (Rev. 10:4; 2 Cor. 12:4). It is complete in the sense that nothing should be added or removed from the Scriptures (Rev. 22:18).

God reveals Himself to us in different ways. He reveals Himself in a general way through history (1 Cor. 10:1-6), our conscience (Rom. 2:14-16), and nature (Ps.

19:1-6; Rom. 1:18-21). He also reveals Himself in a fuller way in the Bible (Deut. 29:29; 2 Peter 1:20-21) and through the life and ministry of Jesus Christ (John 1:14, 18).

God reveals His Word for a purpose. In fact, several things are accomplished through the Scriptures. Scriptures reveal our sin (Rom. 3:9-20). They reveal Christ (John 5:39; Rev. 1:1). They reveal how we can obtain eternal life (John 20:31; 1 John 5:13). Scriptures also reveal God's expectations in our life (2 Tim. 3:17). Further, Scriptures reveal the keys to both wisdom (Prov. 1:2, 5; Ps. 19:7) and spiritual victory (Ps. 119:9-11; Eph. 6:16-17).

How God Wrote the Bible

Evangelical Christians have a high view of the Bible and recognize it as the "inspired" Word of God. The term "inspiration" is based on the Greek word *theopneustos* which communicates the idea of God "breathing out" His Word (2 Tim. 3:16). The Bible teaches that "holy men of God spake as they were moved by the Holy Ghost" (1 Peter 1:21). Our understanding of inspiration is that the Holy Spirit guided human authors so that what they wrote in Scripture is accurate and without error.

Although the individual books of the Bible bear the marks of the personalities of the human authors, God so moved these writers that the very words of Scripture are those "which the Holy Ghost teacheth" (1 Cor. 2:13). Because God is the ultimate author of all Scripture, all Scripture is completely accurate and reliable.

The writer to the Hebrews began his epistle by reminding his readers that God "at sundry times and in divers manners spake in time past unto the fathers by the prophets" (Heb. 1:1). Some of the ways God spoke included dreams (Dan. 7:1), visions (Ezek. 1:1), an audible voice (Lev. 1:1), object lessons (Jer. 19:1-15), dictation (Rev. 2:1-3:22), eyewitness reports (1 John 1:1-3), and historical research (Luke 1:1-4). But even though different methods were used to reveal different parts of Scripture, every verse is as inspired as every other verse.

The divine inspiration of the Scriptures is best recognized by reading the Scriptures. Just as the character of an author tends to come through in his or her writing, so the character of God is reflected on every page of Scripture. Both God and His Book, the Bible, may be described as holy (Isa. 6:3; Ps. 119:3), true (John 17:3, 17), just (1 John 1:9; Ps. 119:149), powerful (Nah. 1:2; Heb. 4:12), and eternal (Ps. 90:2; Matt. 24:35). In fact, every attribute of God is reflected to some degree in the pages of Scripture.

When New Testament writers described the Scriptures as inspired, they were most often speaking of the Old Testament. Still, there is some evidence that they quickly recognized the inspiration of the New Testament as it was being written. Peter commented on the epistles of Paul in a way that suggests he viewed them as inspired as "the rest of the Scriptures" (2 Peter 3:16). Paul quoted both Deuteronomy 25:4 and Luke 10:7 as Scripture which supported a particular principle he was teaching (1 Tim. 5:18). Some Bible teachers believe John 21:24 was written by the elders of the church at Ephesus to attest to their confidence in the authenticity and inspiration of the fourth gospel.

When we say the Scriptures are inspired, we mean that every word of the original autographs of Scripture is the very word God chose to use. The Scriptures were originally written in Hebrew, Aramaic, and Greek, and have since been translated into hundreds of other languages. Most Bible translators have a high regard for the Scriptures and do their best to accurately translate the Word of God into the language of the people. As we read these translations, we are reading the Word of God and should respond accordingly.

Is the Bible Reliable?

The third word we use to describe the Bible is "inerrancy." Inerrancy literally means "without error." When used to describe the Bible, the term *inerrancy* implies that what God inspired is also authoritative and reliable. This was the view of Paul (2 Tim. 3:16), Peter (Acts 4:24–25), and Jesus (John 10:34–35).

One of the strongest statements concerning biblical inerrancy comes from Jesus Himself. In His Sermon on the Mount, Jesus taught, "Till heaven and earth pass, one jot or one tittle shall in no wise pass from the law, till all be fulfilled" (Matt. 5:18). This verse refers to the Old Testament which was written primarily in the Hebrew language. The word "jot" refers to the Hebrew letter "yodh" which was the smallest letter in that alphabet. Other Hebrew letters are very similar in appearance (i.e. "caph" and "beth"). The otherwise insignificant mark distinguishing these letters is called the "tittle." Jesus believed in inerrancy to the point of the smallest letter and part of a letter. Some English translations use the expression "the dotting of the 'i' and the crossing of the 't' " to convey the meaning of this expression in the English language.

When a person assumes the inerrancy of Scripture, their faith is rewarded many times over. Christopher Columbus read of "the circle of the earth." In his day, people believed the earth was flat. But Columbus had faith in God's Word. As a result, he discovered a new world.

An oil man read of the mother of Moses coating a basket with "pitch" which he knew as a petroleum by-product. He sent prospectors to the Middle East to find the first oil wells in that part of the world.

A British army officer found himself trapped by the enemy in the wilderness of Palestine, but escaped by following the escape route used by David to flee Saul. He found that route by reading His Bible one morning and led those under his command along it, even though the route was not marked on any of his maps.

How God Preserved His Word to Us

One of the unique features of the Scriptures is its continued existence. Perhaps no other book in history has been so vigorously and consistently opposed. The energies of several governments have been focused on destroying the Bible, yet God has preserved His Word to this generation. Most of the great books of antiquity have been lost over the years, yet there are thousands of biblical manuscripts and fragments available to scholars today. Few books published today remain in print for as long as a decade, yet after eighteen centuries the Bible is still widely published, distributed, and read.

When Bible teachers talk about preservation, they refer to God's work of insuring that the Scriptures are preserved for future generations. The doctrine of preservation is a logical conclusion of the doctrines of revelation and inspiration. Since God reveals Himself in the Scriptures He inspired, it is only logical to conclude that he will also preserve those Scriptures for future generations.

The doctrine of preservation is perhaps best illustrated in an event which took place during the life and ministry of the prophet Jeremiah (Jer. 36:1-32). God gave him a message to pass on to the king, but as the king began to hear the message, he cut up the scroll on which it was written and threw it in the fire. Even though the original copy of Jeremiah's prophecies was destroyed, the Lord enabled the prophet to reproduce the message on another scroll to replace the one which had been destroyed. God preserved His Word even though it had been cut up and burned in a fire.

Recognizing the Authority of the Scriptures

Some religious groups recognize the Bible as one of several holy books or scriptures. They claim God has spoken through the Vedic Scriptures or Book of Morman just as He has spoken through the Bible. Evangelical Christians reject that claim because they believe the sixty-six books of the Bible form the completed canon of Scripture. We use the word "canonicity" to describe those books which are included in the Bible because they measure up to the standard of Scripture.

The word canon originally meant *a measuring rod* or *standard of measure*. It was applied to the Old Testament as Jewish leaders determined which books should or should not be viewed as Scripture. According to the Jewish historian Josephus, the thirty-nine books of the Old Testament were brought together during the life of Ezra (Neh. 8:1). The Old Testament canon was well established by the time of Jesus. Evangelical Christians have followed the example of Jesus and recognize the canonicity of the Old Testament.

The early church used four criteria to determine the canonicity of a New Testament book. First, each book was written by an apostle or one closely associated with an apostle. Second, the contents of these books were revelatory in nature. Third, these books were universally recognized by the church in their teaching and preaching ministry. Fourth, these books were considered inspired because they bore the marks of inspiration. When the twenty-seven books of the New Testament were gathered into the canon, the Scriptures were complete.

There are several reasons we believe there will be no additions to the books of Scripture that we consider canonical. Scripture forbids adding or removing anything from itself (Rev. 22:18-19). The task of writing revelation is completed and we now have "the faith which was once for all delivered to the saints" (Jude 3). The prophetic and apostolic offices of the early church no longer exist, therefore no one is qualified to write additional Scripture (Eph. 2:20). The widespread acceptance of the Bible among spiritual people as the only authoritative Scripture for Christians is also an indication that only the Bible is in fact God's Word (1 Cor. 3:6-9; John 10:24).

How God Makes the Bible Come Alive

Bible teachers use the word "illumination" to describe the work of the Holy Spirit which enables us to understand and apply the spiritual message of the Scriptures. When Jesus met two disciples on the Emmaus Road, "He expounded to them in all the Scriptures the things concerning Himself" (Luke 24:27). Later, "their eyes were opened and they knew Him" (Luke 24:31). In illumination, the Holy Spirit opens our eyes so that we may know the Scriptures.

Illumination is a ministry of the Holy Spirit Who is given "that we might know the things that are freely given to us of God" (1 Cor. 2:12). When the Holy Spirit does this work in our life, it results in our gaining a fuller understanding of the Scriptures (John 16:13-15; 1 Cor. 2:12-16). The illuminating work of the Holy Spirit depends on our relationship with God. Sin can hinder our understanding of Scripture. Like David, we need to pray, "Open thou mine eyes, that I may behold wondrous things out of thy law" (Ps. 119:18).

We cannot understand the Scriptures apart from the Holy Spirit's work of illumination. This is because our spiritual eyes are blinded so that we cannot see the things of God. The Bible speaks of the judicial blindness of Israel brought on by their rejection of Christ (Rom. 11:25), the blindness of hatred (1 John 2:11), the blindness of Gentiles who had not yet been exposed to the light of the Gospel (Isa. 9:2), the inability to see the kingdom of God apart from the new birth (John 3:3), and the work of Satan in blinding people to the Gospel today (2 Cor. 4:3-4).

When the Holy Spirit illuminates the Scriptures, two things happen. First, unsaved people are convicted of their sin (John 16:8). The word "convict" is derived from a Latin expression which means "cause to see." Second, Christians gain a greater understanding of the Scriptures. Spiritual illumination is also called the anointing of the Holy Spirit (1 John 2:20, 27).

As you study the Bible, make full use of the spiritual principles of interpreting the Bible. Pray as you study the Scriptures, asking God to help you understand His Word (Ps. 119:33-34). Seek cleansing from all known sin in your life (1 John 1:9). Rely on other Scriptures to help you understand what you are reading, "comparing spiritual things with spiritual" (1 Cor. 2:13).

Interpreting the Meaning of Scripture

The Bible is a spiritual book which must be spiritually discerned, hence the need for illumination. But it is also a book originally written in language most people could understand. However, today many people cannot understand the original language. Therefore Scripture has been translated into different languages so more people can understand. Hence the need for interpretation. While we dare not minimize the role of the Holy Spirit in our understanding the Scriptures, neither can we ignore the basic principles of biblical interpretation in this regard either.

Evangelical Christians believe in the "historical grammatical" interpretation of the Bible. This means they interpret the Bible in its historical context using the normal rules of grammar. This involves four steps in the interpretive process.

1. The student of the Bible should learn the context in which the Scripture being read took place.

2. The student should then examine the grammatical context.

3. The student should ask, "What is the literal meaning of this passage?"

4. The student should consider the meaning of idioms and other more figurative expressions in the passage.

Each of these steps helps the student understand what the original writer intended to say and what the original readers interpreted that writer to mean.

Some people tend to get confused in Bible study, largely through their failure to study the Bible as they would study another piece of literature. Don't spend all your time looking for some hidden meaning in Scripture to the point of missing the very obvious. Rather, work on understanding the history and grammar involved, then look for ways to apply what you understand the Bible to be saying.

Applying the Bible to Life

Ultimately, the real value of the Bible is realized in our life as we apply the Scriptures to life. Application is living out the principles taught in the Word of God. God gave us His Word "for doctrine, for reproof, for correction, for instruction in righteousness: that the man of God may be perfect, throughly furnished unto all good works" (2 Tim. 3:16-17). On the flyleaf of his Bible, D. L. Moody wrote the words, "This Book will keep you from sin, or sin will keep you from this Book." If we let it, the Bible can change our life.

Watch out for abuses of Scripture. Admittedly, some rather strange things have been done by those who claim to be "applying the Scriptures." Some people handle snakes, drink poison from mason jars or turn propane torches on themselves during worship services based on their unique interpretation of certain verses. Others have refused medical treatment, abused children, and committed other violent acts to inflict God's judgment upon those they view as sinners. But each of these actions is contrary to the teaching of Scripture.

Before applying Scripture to life, be sure you know what it means. This involves the work of the Holy Spirit in illumination and the work of the Bible student in interpretation (see previous page). Once God has made His will clear through the Scriptures, the Christian needs to obey it. Don't let other people's misapplication of Scripture hinder you in your relationship with the Word of God. Rather, "as newborn babes, desire the sincere milk of the word, that ye may grow thereby" (1 Peter 2:2). And as you study the Bible, "be doers of the word, and not hearers only" (James 1:22).

Chapter One Review & Discussion

Review Questions

1. What eight theme words are related to accepting and understanding the Bible?

2. Why is the Bible the greatest book in the world?

3. What are different ways God reveals himself to us?

4. How did God "write" the Bible.

Discussion Questions

1. Why is the Bible reliable?

2. What would help you understand the Bible better?

3. How can you apply the Bible to your own life?

Chapter Two

CHAPTER TWO

What We Believe about God

"The history of mankind will probably show that no people has ever risen above its religion, and man's spiritual history will positively demonstrate that no religion has ever been greater than its idea about God. Worship is pure or base as the worshiper entertains high or low thoughts of God."[1] This observation by A. W. Tozer helps us understand why it is so important to understand what we believe about God.

Because of the very nature of God, we could never exhaust all there is to learn about Him. In a sense, our understanding of who God is will always be limited. But because God has chosen to reveal Himself to us, there are things we can know about God. As we come to understand these things, our view of God will impact the way we live.

God is the object of our faith as Christians. The writer of the Epistle to the Hebrews noted "he that cometh to God must believe that he is, and that he is a rewarder of them that diligently seek him" (Heb. 11:6). When a missionary was asked, "How can I have greater faith?" the response was, "You don't need a greater faith. You need a greater God." As we grow in our understanding of our great God, our faith in God will also grow.

The Nature of God

One of the most difficult questions to answer concerning God is, "Who is God?" Theologians and philosophers have for generations engaged in long discourses in vain attempts to define "God" adequately. Because people are by nature limited in their understanding and God is by nature without limits, it is probably impossible for us to completely understand the nature of God.

While we may not know everything about the nature of God, there are some things we can know about who God is. Throughout Scripture, God is defined as Spirit, a person, life, self-existent, unchanging, unlimited by time and space, and a unity. To understand God better, it is important to understand these seven aspects of His nature.

GOD IS DEFINED AS
Spirit
A Person
Life
Self-Existent
Unchanging
Unlimited by Time and Space
A Unity

When we acknowledge that God is Spirit (John 4:24), we recognize that God is not limited by a physical body. The word "spirit" means "incorporeal being." God is sometimes described by metaphors of a physical body (hands, Isa. 65:2; feet, Ps. 8:6; eyes, 1 Kings 8:29; and fingers, Ex. 8:19). These expressions describe aspects of God such as His strength, steadfastness or insight rather than providing a physical description of God's "body." Other biblical metaphors describe God as having wings (Ps. 17:8) and feathers (Ps. 91:4), but that does not mean God is a bird. These expressions describe God's care for us comparing it to a hen's care for her chicks.

The Bible describes God as a person, although most of the world's religions tend to portray God as an impersonal being or force. God is described in Scripture as having the characteristics of personality including self-awareness (Ex. 3:14), self-determination (Job 23:13), intelligence (Gen. 18:19), emotion (Ex. 3:7–8), and volition or will (John 4:34).

God is characterized as life in Scripture. One of His many names is "the Living God" (1 Sam. 17:26). He is both the source and sustainer of all life (John 5:26).

One of the primary names of God in the Old Testament, Jehovah, emphasizes the self-existent nature of God. When He described Himself to Moses as "I am that I am" (Ex. 3:13-15), He emphasized the fact that He exists independent of all other things in the universe. Our continued existence depends on the environment which God has placed us in, but God exists without that limitation.

God is immutable or unchanging. Changes either improve or corrupt the person or thing being changed. Since God by definition is perfect (Ps. 102:25-27), any changes in His being would make Him less than perfect. The Bible describes God "changing" in a few places (Gen. 6:6; 1 Sam. 15:11), but in each case the apparent change in God really describes a change in people. God is consistent in His attitude toward sin. When people change by practicing sin or turning from sin, God's consistent response to sin may be perceived as a change in His response to changing people.

God is not limited by time and space. Another of His names is "the Everlasting God" (Gen. 21:33). When Paul described God to the Athenian philosophers, he noted, "God that made the world and all the things therein, seeing that he is Lord of heaven and earth, dwelleth not in temples made with hands" (Acts 17:24). Bible teachers describe this aspect of God's nature as the infinity and immensity of God. It is the foundation of our view of God's sovereignty in the universe.

God is also described as being "one Lord" (Deut. 6:4) – a reflection of His unity. There can only be one God

(Isa. 44:6). Our faith in the Trinity is not inconsistent
with this aspect of God's nature because we believe in
one God in three personalities, not three separate gods.
The biblical teaching concerning the Trinity is discussed
later in this chapter.

The Attributes of God

The Bible describes various attributes of God to help
us understand Him better. An attribute of God may be
described as the virtues or qualities which manifest His
nature. While there are many positive characteristics of
God, six are especially significant. These attributes may
be divided into two groups, the absolute attributes and
comparative attributes of God.

The absolute attributes of God are so named because they are found exclusively in God. These attributes include omniscience (Ps. 139:1-6), omnipresence
(Ps. 139:7-11), and omnipotence (Ps. 139:12-16). While
people have some knowledge, only God has all knowledge (omniscience). Every person has a presence, but
only God is at all times everywhere present (omnipresence). Each of us has some strength, but all power belongs exclusively to God (omnipotence).

While the absolute attributes of God refer to things
true only about God, the comparative attributes of God
describe things which are also true to a much lesser ex-
tent in people. These attributes include holiness, love,
and goodness. While Christians should have a holy lifestyle, love others, and do good deeds, these three attributes exist in their pure form only in God. God is described by His name "Holy" in Scripture (Ps. 111:9; Isa.
57:15). Because God is holy, we also should live holy
lives (Lev. 19:2). God is also described by the statement,
"God is love" (1 John 4:8, 16). Our responsibility to love
one another as Christians is tied to God's demonstration
of love in saving us (1 John 4:11). Also, Jesus noted, "No

one is good but One, that is, God" (Mark 10:18). Because God is good, He has worked in the lives of Christians to equip them to do good works.

The Law of God

God expresses Himself in various ways. The expression of His will is called the law of God. It is the extension of His nature and attributes. Some people describe the law of God as the Ten Commandments or the 632 rules and regulations Moses gave the Jews, but God's law is much broader than that limited description. There are many areas in which God expresses His will.

The Bible describes the natural world as being held together by God (Col. 1:17). The natural law of God is the expression of God's will concerning the means by which He chooses to govern the world He created (Gen. 8:22).

God also expresses His will concerning moral issues touching our life. This is called the moral law of God. Even in the New Testament, specific sins such as lying (Eph. 4:25), theft (Eph. 4:28), gossip (James 4:11), lust (Matt. 5:28), and anger (Matt. 5:22) are prohibited. This aspect of the law of God is reflected in the description of the Bible as "the perfect law of liberty" (James 1:25).

The expression of God's will concerning our relationships with others is called the social law of God. Jewish rabbis divided the Ten Commandments into two groups, noting that the first four describe one's relationship with God while the remaining six describe one's relationship with others. This second group of commandments is also called "the royal law" (James 2:8).

A final aspect of God's law is the spiritual law of God. This is the expression of God's will relating to a person's relationship with Him. Jesus called the command to love God the first and great commandment (Matt. 22:37-38).

The Bible describes the law of God as holy (Rom. 7:12), good (Rom. 7:16), and spiritual (Rom. 7:14). It was given to reveal the nature of God (Ps. 19:7), provide a standard of life (Josh. 1:8), instruct Israel concerning their Messiah (1 Cor. 10:11), reveal sin in our life (Rom. 5:13), and direct us to Christ (Gal. 3:24).

The Work of God

In our worship of God, we praise Him for both who He is and His mighty acts. God consistently works out His eternal plan by guiding and overseeing all things by His wise and holy purpose. Bible teachers refer to these acts as the *work* of God rather than the *works* of God because they fit into a single eternal and unchangeable plan, that all come to salvation through faith in God.

The work of God is based upon God's sovereignty. The Scriptures teach that: Salvation begins with the initiative of God, yet people are also responsible to respond (2 Thess. 2:13-14). God's work is based on His wisdom (Rom. 11:33). God's work is consistent with His nature (Isa. 40:13-14). God's work is committed to glorify God (Eph. 1:6). God's work is both active and passive.

The Bible describes God at work in the physical, social, and spiritual dimensions of our life. God created and sustains the physical world in which we live (Ps. 33:6-11). Also, He has ordained several social institutions which are foundational to our society, including the family (Gen. 2:24), the church (Matt. 16:18), and civil government (Rom. 13:1-7). Ultimately, the work of God is expressed in our salvation in two ways. First, He has provided the means whereby all people may be saved. Second, He calls specific individuals to communicate the message of salvation to others.

The Trinity

Perhaps the most difficult-to-understand aspect of the doctrine of God is the doctrine of the Trinity. Yet this is at the very heart of Christian doctrine. When Christians describe God as a Trinity, they mean that He exists in unity in three eternal persons. Each member of the Trinity is equal in nature, yet distinct in person and submissive in duties. While each person of the Trinity is equally God, each has voluntarily adopted subservient roles. The Son is eternally begotten by the Father (Ps. 2:7). The Holy Spirit is described as proceeding from the Father and the Son (John 15:26).

Sometimes it is easier to understand what is not meant by the expression *Trinity*. The Trinity is not equivalent to three Gods (tritheism). Also, the Trinity is not three manifestations of God (the Father who becomes the Son who becomes the Holy Spirit). Nor does this doctrine teach that the Father created either the Son or the Holy Spirit. Further, the Trinity does not describe the Son or the Holy Spirit as mere attributes of the Father.

Some who oppose this doctrine claim it is not supported in the Old Testament. Actually, the Old Testament implies this doctrine by using a plural name for God (Elohim), using a Trinitarian formula in the worship of God (Isa. 6:3; Num. 6:24-26), and describing three distinct persons as God (Gen. 19:24; Isa. 9:6; Gen. 1:2). But the Old Testament goes farther than merely implying this doctrine. On at least one occasion, Father, Son, and Holy Spirit are referred to in the context of deity in a single verse (Isa. 48:16).

This doctrine is more fully described in the New Testament. The Trinity was apparent at the baptism of Jesus when the Spirit descended like a dove and the Father spoke (Matt. 3:16-17). Jesus taught the Trinity when He spoke of sending the Holy Spirit from the Father (John 15:26). In the early church, each member of the Trinity was named in the apostolic benediction (2 Cor. 13:14) and the baptismal formula (Matt. 28:19). Also, the atoning death of Christ was understood by the early church in the context of each member of the Trinity being involved in offering the ultimate sacrifice for sin.

The Names of God

God teaches us who He is by revealing His nature in His names. In many cultures, a name is given to a person to describe their character or the aspirations of parents to see certain character developed in the life of their children. Throughout the Scriptures, God is described by various names and titles which emphasize specific things which are true about God.

There are many names of God in Scripture. This is because there is much we can know about God. Also, since God relates to His people in so many different ways, there are many names that describe His relationships with people. The significant names of God in the Old Testament tend to fall into two groups. First, the primary names of God are so named because they stand alone in describing God. The compound names of God are derived from the primary names and describe God in a more specific way.

There are three primary names of God in Scripture. The name Elohim, translated "God," is by far the most-often-used name of God. This name describes God as the Strong One who manifests Himself by His Word. This is both the first and last name of God used in Scripture (Gen. 1:1; Rev. 22:19). The name Jehovah (translated LORD) is sometimes called the covenant name of God because it is most often used in a context of God relating to His people. It is based on the verb "to be" and may be translated "I am" or "I will become." Some Bible teachers see this name as a promise that God "will become" what is needed most in the life of His people. The third primary name of God is Adonai which means Lord or Master. This name tends to emphasize the authority of God over that which He possesses.

The compound names of God are composed of a primary name of God and a verb or descriptive phrase about the nature of God. The compound names of Elohim include El Shaddai which is translated the Almighty God or All-sufficient God (Gen. 17:1–2), El Elyon which describes God as the Most High God who possesses heaven and earth (Gen. 14:18, 22), and El Olam who is the Everlasting God (Gen. 21:33). The compound names of Jehovah include Jehovah Sabaoth (the LORD of Hosts - Ps. 24:10), Jehovah Jireh (the LORD will Provide - Gen. 22:14), Jehovah Rapha (the LORD that Heals - Ex. 15:26), Jehovah Nissi (the LORD our Banner - Ex. 17:15), Jehovah Shalom (the LORD our Peace - Judg. 6:24), and Jehovah Rohi (the LORD my Shepherd - Ps. 23:1).

There are many other names of God used in Scripture, too many to even list in this chapter.[2] Each of these names tells us something unique about God which we could not otherwise have known. As we learn more about God, we should be eager to let that knowledge change our life. The more we know about who God is and how He relates to us, the more we will be able to trust Him and worship Him for who He is.

1 A.W. Tozer, *The Knowledge of the Holy* (New York: Harper & Row, Publishers, 1975), page 9.

2 See Elmer L. Towns, *My Father's Names* (Ventura, California: Regal Books, 1991) for a more complete study of the names of God in the Old Testament.

Chapter Two Review & Discussion

Review Questions

1. What are seven aspects of God's nature?

2. What is the difference between absolute attributes and comparative attributes?

3. What is the "law of God"?

4. What is the "work of God"?

Discussion Questions

1. Describe the Trinity.

2. Why is God referred to by so many different names in Scripture?

3. Why should we learn more about who God is and how He relates to us?

Chapter Three

CHAPTER THREE

What We Believe about Christ

No other single individual has impacted the history of the world in general and western civilization in particular more than Jesus of Nazareth. This humble son of a carpenter lived most of His life in obscurity spending little more than three years in the public limelight as a popular teacher of religious truth. He was eventually executed to appease the religious leaders of His day who could not refute Him and would not endorse Him. Yet His death marked the beginning of a new dimension of His influence rather than the end of His movement. In spite of incredible opposition directed at His movement throughout history, vast multitudes of people continue to follow Him today.

Here is what the Jewish historian Josephus wrote about Jesus, "Now, there as about this time Jesus, a wise man, if it be lawful to call him a man, for he was a doer of wonderful works; a teacher of such men as receive the truth with pleasure. He drew over to him both many of the Jews, and many of the Gentiles. He was [the] Christ; and when Pilate, at the suggestion of the principal men amongst us, had condemned him to the cross, those that loved him at the first did not forsake him; for he appeared to them alive again the third day, as the divine prophets had foretold these and ten thousand other wonderful things concerning him; and the tribe of Christians, so named from him, are not extinct at this day."[1]

Obviously, Jesus of Nazareth was more than the son of a carpenter. The Bible teaches us that Jesus was in fact God incarnate in human form. He is the second person in the Trinity who came to live among us, die for us, and resurrect that someday we might be able to live with Him forever. In many respects, what we believe about Jesus impacts the very heart of our Christian life.

The life of Jesus Christ is the focus of all God has revealed about Jesus. In the Old Testament, the prophets described Christ in types and prophecies anticipating His coming. In the New Testament, the epistles describe the implications of His life in the context of the Christian life. During His life and ministry on earth, Jesus promised He would return a second time at the end of the age (see chapter eight). The fulfillment of prophecy associated with the first coming of Christ gives us reason for the hope in His return.

Six significant aspects in Jesus Christ's life and ministry illustrate something of His uniqueness. These aspects include the Incarnation, the Atonement, the Resurrection, the Ascension, His present ministry, and His involvement in Christian life. These six themes summarize what we believe about Jesus.

The Incarnation

The birth of Jesus may be the most familiar aspect of the life of Jesus to many people. During the Christmas season, many people take time out of their schedules to reflect on the appearance of angels and coming of shepherds to a stable in Bethlehem. They exchange cards with Christmas greetings and pictures of wise men and nativity scenes. When they attend a church service on Christmas Sunday or Christmas Eve, they are again reminded of some of the historical details surrounding His birth. But often, their understanding of Christmas fails to penetrate beyond the obvious to discover the real meaning of what happened at Christmas.

The Apostle John described that first Christmas with these words, "And the Word was made flesh and dwelt among us" (John 1:14). This brief statement describes what Bible teachers call "the Incarnation." This word is used to describe God becoming a man, taking on human flesh. The mystery of the Incarnation implies several things about Jesus. First, it implies a pre-existence of Christ prior to His birth. Second, it suggests some voluntary limitations of Christ as God during His life and ministry. Third, it explains why Jesus was necessarily born of a virgin rather than through the normal biological means of reproduction. Fourth, it serves as the basis for understanding the human and divine natures of Christ.

As the Second Person of the Trinity, Jesus lived long before His physical "birth" in Bethlehem. Jesus existed with God from the beginning (John 1:1). Throughout the Old Testament, there are various appearances of God to men. Bible teachers refer to these appearances as Christophanies because they were preincarnate appearances of Christ. The very fact that Jesus is God demands His existence from eternity to eternity (Ps. 90:1).

But how could the Eternal God take on human flesh? The answer to that question is found in what Bible teachers call "the kenosis." *Kenosis* is a Greek word which means "emptied." The apostle Paul used this word to describe Jesus emptying Himself to become a man (Phil. 2:7). Jesus remained God, but He emptied himself by veiling his glory, accepting the limitations of being a human, and voluntarily giving up the independent use of His relative attributes. Even though John saw the glory of Jesus during his years with his Master (John 1:14), it was a veiled glory. Later, on the island of Patmos, John saw Jesus in His resurrected glory and "fell at His feet as dead" (Rev. 1:17). Although Jesus performed miracles, He was also subject to human limitations and experienced things like hunger (Matt. 4:2) and thirst (John 4:6). Even in doing miracles, He relied on the power of the Holy Spirit to do the will of His Father (John 5:19).

Why was Jesus willing to empty Himself, setting aside all that was rightfully His to become a man? There are several reasons which may have motivated Him in this act. First, the act of sacrifice was an act of love (John 15:13). Because He loved us, He was prepared to become a man and go to the Cross even when we continued to reject Him (Rom. 5:8). Second, this was the best way He could reveal His Father to us (John 1:14, 18; 14:7-11). Third, it was the only way He could provide salvation to counter the effects of Adam's sin (Rom. 5:12-21). Finally, He humbled Himself as an example for us to follow (Phil. 2:5).

When we understand the deity of Jesus – that He is God – it becomes easier to understand why He was miraculously conceived in a virgin. When the human race fell into sin, God offered hope in "the seed of the woman" (Gen. 3:15). Later, Isaiah prophesied, "Behold, the virgin shall conceive and bear a Son, and shall call His name Immanuel" (Isa. 7:14). In the New Testament, Matthew, Luke, and Paul each describe the Virgin Birth of Jesus (Matt. 1:25; Luke 1:27; 3:23; Gal. 4:4).

The result of the Virgin Birth is that Jesus was born with the human nature of His mother and the divine nature of His Father. He did not inherit a sin nature that we inherit from our fathers because His Father was God. The Scriptures are very clear concerning Christ and His absence of sin. Christ knew no sin (2 Cor. 5:2), was without sin (Heb. 4:15), did no sin (1 Pet. 2:22), and there was no sin found in Him (1 John 3:5).

When Christian leaders tried to explain the human and divine natures of Jesus at the Council of Chalcedon in A.D. 451, they issued a statement which described Jesus as "made known in two natures without confusion, without change, without division, without separation, the distinction of natures being by no means taken away by the union." When Jesus became a man, He remained

God while also becoming human. Neither of these natures was in any way corrupted or altered in the process.

The Bible has several things to say about this unique union of two natures. Jesus was both completely human and completely divine. This union of natures was complete, not partial, and was permanent (Heb. 13:8). Finally, this union of natures has continued beyond the resurrection of Christ. Today, "the man Christ Jesus" acts as our mediator before God the Father (1 Tim. 2:5).

The incarnation of Christ gives special meaning and significance to Christmas. The Christmas season celebrates the moment in human history when "the Word became flesh" to confirm God's promises (Rom. 15:8; Matt. 5:17), reveal the Father (John 1:18), become a faithful high priest (Heb. 5:1; 7:25), put away sin (Gen. 22:8; John 1:29), destroy the works of Satan (1 John 3:8), and provide an example for us to follow (1 John 2:6; 1 Peter 2:21).

The Atonement

The second key significant event in Christ's life was His atoning death. His death is commemorated annually in Good Friday services around the world. As is the case with His birth, various historical details concerning the death of Jesus are well known by many people. But many of those same people do not understand the special significance God attached to the death of Jesus. Many view His death as that of a martyr who died for a noble cause, but the Bible describes His death as having a greater significance than mere martyrdom.

Bible teachers use the word *atonement* to describe the character of Jesus' death. The word atonement literally means "covering" and is used in the Old Testament to describe the limited covering of sins accomplished by animal sacrifices. When applied to the death of Christ, this word has a much broader meaning and describes that which was accomplished by His death. Those accomplishments may be summarized by the words substitution, redemption, propitiation, and reconciliation.

The Bible teaches that Christ's death was substitutionary in nature. Under the Old Testament law, animals were sacrificed as substitutes for people who were sinners. Jesus fulfilled this aspect of the sacrifice by dying as a substitute for Christians (2 Cor. 5:21; Rom. 5:8), the church (Eph. 5:25), and for every person (Heb. 2:9). Christ's death was also redemptive in nature. The word redemption means "to purchase." The apostle Paul uses three different Greek words to describe the redemptive nature of Christ's death. First, the word *agorazo* means "to purchase in the market" (Gal. 3:10). This word describes Jesus purchasing us in the slave market of sin just as people purchased slaves in the first century slave markets. Second, the word *ekagorazo* means "to purchase out and take home" (Gal. 3:13). This word describes our being purchased and removed from the marketplace, never again to be sold into sin. Third, the word *lutroo* means "to purchase and give freedom" (Titus 2:14). This word describes our being purchased as slaves and granted liberty as free persons (Gal. 5:1).

The third word describing Christ's death is "propitiation." This is a technical term refering to sacrificial offering that appeased or satisfied God (Rom. 3:25; 1 John 4:10). Christ's death was propitious in two senses. It satisfied God who is the One ultimately offended by sin (1 John 2:2). It satisfied the demands of the law which is violated when we sin (Eph. 2:15; Col. 2:14).

The fourth accomplishment in Christ's death was the reconciliation of the world to God (2 Cor. 5:19). Sin made us the enemies of God, but in His death Christ made it possible for us to become friends of God. The Cross was the means of removing the enmity between God and people (Eph. 2:16). When we come to Christ for salvation, we are placed "in Christ" (Gal. 2:20) and He acts as our mediator (1 Tim. 2:5). When God looks at us, He sees His Son. Therefore, we are presented as savable sinners.

The Resurrection of Christ

At the very heart of the Christian Gospel is the miracle of the resurrection of Christ. Although Jesus was certified dead and buried according to the custom of His time, three days later He was seen alive. Ever since that first resurrection Sunday, people who oppose Christianity have tried to explain it away (Matt. 28:11-15). Yet when the known facts of history are examined closely, there can be no other explanation apart from the Resurrection.

Sometimes we hear stories of people who were declared dead, then revived. With advances in medical technology today, these revivings are sometimes possible within minutes of a person's death. But the resurrection of Jesus was more than a reviving of the physical body. First, the resurrection involved a renewing of life that would never end (Acts 2:24). Second, it involved the reunion of the body and spirit. It is not certain that the body and spirit of those who are revived medically were actually separated (James 2:26). Third, His resurrection subjected the power of death (1 Cor. 15:54-55). Fourth, it returned Jesus to the glory which was rightfully His (Heb. 7:24; Rev. 5:7-14). Fifth, the resurrection of Christ is the basis upon which He grants spiritual life to believers (Rom. 6:4; Eph. 1:19-20). Finally, when Jesus was resurrected, He received a glorified body (1 Cor. 15:42-44).

Because Jesus rose from the dead, there are several
benefits He is able to pass on to Christians. These benefits include eternal life (Rom. 6:23), spiritual power
(Eph. 1:19–20), justification (Rom. 4:25), future resurrection (1 Cor. 15:12), and the believer's union with
Christ as the basis of the victorious Christian life (Gal.
2:20).

The Ascension of Christ

Several weeks after His resurrection, Jesus ascended to His Father in heaven. This ascension marked
the end of Christ's self-limitations, the glorification of
Christ (Heb. 12:2), the exaltation of Christ (Acts 2:36),
the entrance of humanity into heaven (Heb. 7:24), and
the beginning of Christ's new ministry as our advocate
(1 John 2:2) and intercessor (Heb. 7:25).

Jesus told His disciples, "It is expedient for you that
I go away" (John 16:7). When Jesus ascended into heav-
en, He was able to send the Holy Spirit (John 16:7), give
spiritual gifts (Eph. 4:8), impart spiritual power (Acts
1:8), prepare our heavenly home (John 14:3), insure the
standing of believers in heaven (Eph. 2:6), and prepare
His throne in heaven (Rev. 11:15).

The Present Ministry of Christ

Today, Jesus continues His ministry to us in two
specific areas. He is described as both our intercessor
(Heb. 7:25) and our advocate (1 John 2:1). While some
Bible teachers choose not to distinguish between these
two words, a distinction does exist. As our intercessor,
Jesus prays for us that we may be able to overcome sin
and live victoriously. When we do fail, He then acts as
our advocate and defends us as sinners by confessing
our guilt and noting that payment for sin has already
been made in His death. Because of the way we live the
Christian life, Jesus is continually acting both as our intercessor and advocate.

Christ and the Christian Life

Christ has not limited Himself to this unique ministry in heaven alone. The Bible also describes Him living in the believer (Gal. 2:20). The indwelling presence of Jesus in the believer is the basis for a victorious Christian life and effective ministry. *Living for and serving Christ is not so much what we do for Him, but rather what we allow Him to do through us.* As we yield more fully to Christ and let Him work in and through us, we will be more effective in both living the victorious Christian life and accomplishing His will in our life.

---

1 *The Works of Flavius Josephus,* translated by William Whiston, M.A. Boston: Dewolfe, Fiske and Company, 1883. Page 474.

Chapter Three Review & Discussion

Review Questions

1. What are Christ's unique aspects?

2. What does Incarnation mean?

3. What is the result of the Virgin Birth?

4. What is significant about Christ's death and resurrection?

Discussion Questions

1. Where would we be without Christ's resurrection?

2. What benefits have you experienced as a result of accepting Christ?

3. How can you live for Christ?

Chapter Four

CHAPTER FOUR

What We Believe about the Holy Spirit

Someone once called the Holy Spirit, "the forgotten person of the Trinity." While that may have been true throughout much of church history, we are living in a generation that has rediscovered the important role of the Holy Spirit in our life. One of the most significant consequences of this awakening is many Christians' interest in discovering and using their spiritual gifts in ministry.

Understanding who the Holy Spirit is, what He does, how we relate to Him, and what He expects of us in our life is important for Christians. As we look at what we believe about the Holy Spirit, we will consider the personality and deity of the Holy Spirit, His ministry in bringing us to Christ and salvation, what He does when we become a Christian, how the Holy Spirit has equipped us for ministry, how we can be empowered for ministry through the fullness of the Holy Spirit, and the spiritual fruit the Holy Spirit produces in our life.

Who Is the Holy Spirit?

Some people view the Holy Spirit mystically, considering Him to be some kind of force or emanation from God. But the Bible teaches that the Holy Spirit is far more than this. He is not merely a force but a person with all the attributes of personality. But neither is the Holy Spirit only a person. Scripture makes it clear that the Holy Spirit is also God.

Personality involves intellect, emotions, and will. The Holy Spirit knows things that only God knows (1 Cor. 2:11). He is also identified as loving (Rom. 15:30) and subject to grief (Eph. 4:30). He also acts on the basis of decisions He makes (1 Cor. 12:11). He is described in Scripture as teaching (John 14:26), testifying (John 15:26), guiding (Rom. 8:14), speaking (1 Cor. 2:13), enlightening (John 16:13), striving (Gen. 6:3), commanding (Acts 8:28), interceding (Rom. 8:26), sending workers (Acts 13:4), calling (Rev. 22:17), comforting (John 16:7), and working (1 Cor. 12:11).

The early church recognized the personality of the Holy Spirit and responded appropriately. They obeyed Him (Acts 10:19), followed His leading (Acts 8:39), and warned others against resisting the Holy Spirit (Acts 7:51). They associated the Holy Spirit with the other two persons of the Trinity when they baptized converts (Matt. 28:19) and blessed one another (2 Cor. 13:14).

Scripture also describes the Holy Spirit as God. Many of the more than one hundred names and titles of the Holy Spirit in Scripture describe Him in divine terms (God, Acts 5:4; Spirit of God, Gen. 1:2; and Spirit of the Lord God, Isa. 61:1). Other names such as Eternal Spirit (Heb. 9:14), Spirit of Truth (John 16:13), and Holy One (1 John 2:20) describe the Holy Spirit as possessing attributes belonging to God. Also, the Holy Spirit is described as accomplishing the work of God in creation (Job. 26:13), regeneration (John 3:5), and inspiration (2 Peter 1:21). There is little question concerning the deity of the Holy Spirit.

The Holy Spirit in the World

Concerning the Holy Spirit, Jesus taught, "And when He has come, He will reprove the world of sin, and of righteousness, and of judgment" (John 16:8). This verse describes the first aspect of the present work of the Holy Spirit in the world. The Holy Spirit convicts of sin "because they do not believe in" Jesus (John 16:9). The Holy Spirit convicts of righteousness because Jesus is no longer living among us to model true righteousness

(John 16:10). The Spirit also convicts people of the reality of the coming judgment upon sin (John 16:11).

A second aspect of the present work of the Holy Spirit in the world is that of restraining evil. It is sometimes hard for Christians to believe sin is restrained at all in this present age, but the Bible describes the Holy Spirit as the Restrainer (2 Thess. 2:7). Sometimes, the presence of a church in the community or a Christian in the office causes people to think twice about doing something wrong. While sin is rampant in our world today, the Bible teaches that things would be far worse without the restraining influence of the Holy Spirit. During times of revival when the presence of the Holy Spirit is widely recognized, a noticeable drop in crime has been recorded and the general quality of life in an area has been improved.

The Holy Spirit in Salvation

In addition to His general work of reproof and restraint in the world, the Holy Spirit is also involved in saving people. The Holy Spirit's work in salvation can be remembered by the acrostic RIBS, representing **Re**generation, **I**ndwelling, **B**aptism, and **S**ealing. *Regeneration* is the work of the Spirit of God whereby we are given God's life and nature and are made a part of the family of God (Tit. 3:5). *Indwelling* is when the Holy Spirit lives within us thus making our bodies the temple of God (1 Cor. 6:19). The *baptism* of the Holy Spirit is when we are placed into our new position "in Christ" as we are "baptized into one body" (1 Cor. 12:13). The *sealing* of the Holy Spirit guarantees that God will complete the work He has begun in our life (Eph. 1:13–14).

These four areas describe things that happen in a person's life as he or she becomes a Christian. But as

Christians our relationship with the Holy Spirit should not be understood exclusively in the past tense. God wants us to enjoy the ministry of the Holy Spirit in at least three areas of our Christian life. First, the Holy Spirit has granted every Christian one or more spiritual gifts which can and should be used in meaningful ministry. Second, we should be filled with the Holy Spirit, allowing the Holy Spirit to control our life more fully (Eph. 5:18). Third, as we mature in Christ, we need to allow the Holy Spirit to produce spiritual fruit in our life.

The Gifts of the Holy Spirit

The apostle Paul used five different Greek words to describe spiritual gifts (1 Cor. 12:1-7). *Pneumatikon* (spiritual) describes the character of these gifts as spiritual (1 Cor. 12:1). *Charismata* (gifts) emphasizes God's free and gracious gifts (1 Cor. 12:4). *Diakonia* (ministries) describes gifts as opportunities for ministry (1 Cor. 12:5). *Energama* (activities) suggests that gifts are an endowment of God's power or energy (1 Cor. 12:6). *Phanerosis* (manifestation) describes gifts as an evidence of God working through us (1 Cor. 12:7).

There are three types of spiritual gifts. The miraculous gifts include such gifts as tongues and healing. The four enabling gifts, which each Christian appears to have to some degree, include discernment, faith, knowledge, and wisdom. These gifts enhance the task-oriented gifts (TEAM gifts). There are nine task-oriented gifts: evangelism (Eph. 4:11), prophecy (Rom. 12:6), teaching (Rom. 12:7), exhortation (Rom. 12:8), shepherding (Eph. 4:11), showing mercy (Rom. 12:8), serving (Rom. 12:7; 1 Cor. 12:28), giving (Rom. 12:8), and administration (Rom. 12:8; 1 Cor. 12:28).

Evangelism is communicating the Gospel in the power of the Holy Spirit to unconverted persons at their point of need with the intent of effecting conversions. These conversions take place as individuals repent of their sin and put their trust in God through Jesus Christ, to accept Him as their Saviour. Normally, people who are converted determine to serve the Lord in the fellowship of a local church. Those who are gifted in evangelism are effective in making disciples of various types of people through their personal evangelistic efforts.

Prophecy is communicating and applying biblical truth to a specific situation or circumstance. An individual with the gift of prophecy "speaketh unto men to edification, and exhortation, and comfort" (1 Cor. 14:3) through exercising this gift. This gift appears to involve some measure of the enabling gift of faith (Rom. 12:6). Christians gifted in this area are usually able to discern problems and apply appropriate biblical principles to help alleviate the problems.

Teaching is communicating biblical principles in the power of the Holy Spirit to others and demonstrating how those principles relate to the specific needs represented. Christians gifted in the area of teaching tend to be diligent students of the Scripture, who have accumulated a thorough understanding of biblical principles as a result of their consistent study habits.

Exhortation is urging others to act on the basis of their faith in God, advising others how to accomplish specific goals in life and ministry, cautioning others against actions that are potentially dangerous, and motivating others in the Christian life and ministry. Those gifted in exhortation usually develop simple strategies to accomplish goals and effectively encourage and motivate others to remain faithful in their service for God.

Pastoring/Shepherding is compassionately caring for others in your sphere of influence through providing spiritual guidance, nourishment, and protection from potentially destructive individuals or influences. Those who have this gift readily express their concern for others and are often looked to for spiritual counsel and guidance.

Showing mercy is discovering emotionally stressed and distressed individuals and ministering to their emotional needs. Mercy-showers express sympathy, empathy, and spiritual ministry to help alleviate the inner pain that is causing a person's dysfunctional emotional response. Those gifted in showing mercy tend to be drawn toward hurting people and are somewhat effective in helping others rebuild their lives.

Serving is discerning and meeting the spiritual and physical needs of individuals. Those gifted in this ministry support others and are concerned with helping them in any way possible. They often enjoy manual tasks.

Giving is investing financial and other resources in ways that further the purposes of God through individuals and/or ministries. Givers are inclined to be generous in financially underwriting a wide variety of ministry projects.

Administration is the management of human, physical, and financial resources through planning, organizing, leading, and controlling. Planning involves projecting the future, establishing objectives, developing policies, programs, procedures, and schedules for accomplishing these objectives, and budgeting adequate resources for the task. Organization involves developing an organizational foundation, delegating responsibilities, and establishing interpersonal relationships. Leading involves making decisions, communicating ideas, and selecting, enlisting, training, and motivating people. Controlling involves establishing performance standards, then measuring, evaluating, and correcting performance on the basis of those standards. People who are gifted in administration are effective managers.

In light of the Holy Spirit's work in giving us spiritual gifts, it is important for every Christian to discover their spiritual gift, demonstrate it in ministry, and develop it to its fullest potential.

There are several ways Christians can discover their spiritual giftedness. First, they can use a Spiritual Gifts Inventory to help them identify areas in which they are probably gifted.[1] Second, they can look at their personal ministry passion as an indicator of probable giftedness in that area. Third, they can compare themselves to a standard profile of a person gifted in some area to note areas of similarity.

Once you have identified your spiritual gift, you should begin using it in ministry. Many churches experience a shortage of workers because church members do not use their gifts in ministry. By simply calling the church office, most Christians can quickly learn of several ministry opportunities available for utilizing their gift.

Your involvement in ministry will motivate you to develop your giftedness further. Every Christian needs to continually learn more about his or her spiritual gift and develop gift-related ministry skills to increase his or her effectiveness. You can begin today by looking for articles, books, seminars, workshops, and other learning experiences to help you develop your spiritual gift(s).

The Fulness of the Holy Spirit

Many Christians have different ideas about the fulness of the Holy Spirit. In the New Testament, the fulness of the Holy Spirit was sometimes associated with cloven tongues of fire, shaking buildings, rushing winds, and people speaking in other languages or doing miracles. At other times, people were filled with the Holy Spirit and none of these things happened. According to the Bible, there appear to be two evidences that a person is indeed filled with the Spirit. First, those who are filled with the Holy Spirit have unique spiritual power in leading others to faith in Christ (Acts 1:8). Second, those who are filled with the Holy Spirit have a divine enablement to fulfill their social roles and responsibilities, particularly in family and working relationships (Eph. 5:18–6:9).

Most Christians readily recognize their need to be filled with the Holy Spirit to become more effective in evangelism and be all they should be in their family. The apostle Paul urged the Christians at Ephesus, "Be filled with the Spirit" (Eph. 5:18). But the steps to being filled with the Holy Spirit were summarized by Jesus when He said, "If any man thirst, let him come unto me, and drink. He that believeth on me, as the scripture hath said, out of his belly (heart) shall flow rivers of living water" (John 7:37-38). The four steps to being filled with the Holy Spirit are (1) desire (thirst), (2) repentance of all known sin in your life (come to me), (3) receiving God's offer of the Holy Spirit to those who obey Him (drink), and (4) acting on the basis of faith in the Word of God (He who believeth in me).

The Fruit of the Holy Spirit

As you live your Christian life in the fulness of the Holy Spirit, you will encourage the Holy Spirit to produce spiritual fruit in your life. The Bible describes the fruit of the Spirit as the character traits of love, joy, peace, longsuffering, kindness, goodness, faithfulness, gentleness, and self-control (Gal. 5:22-23). Producing spiritual fruit in our lives is one of the primary means by which the Holy Spirit continually transforms us into the image of Christ (Phil. 1:6; Rom. 8:29).

Chapter Four Review & Discussion

Review Questions

1. What is the Holy Spirit's present work?

2. Describe the Holy Spirit's role in salvation.

3. What are the nine task-oriented spiritual gifts?

Discussion Questions

1. How can you discover your own spiritual gift(s)?

2. What should you do after determining your gift(s)?

3. What spiritual fruits are evident in your life?

---

1 Church Growth Institute (CGI) offers the best-selling Spiritual Gifts Inventory in this country. It is available separately or with *TEAM Ministry,* a practical study of spiritual gifts. *TEAM Ministry* is available from CGI as a complete resource packet of leadership planning and teaching materials or the text may be purchased separately.

Chapter Five

CHAPTER FIVE

What We Believe about People

People are unique beings in all of God's creation. The Bible teaches that God created man out of the dust of the ground and gave him life by personally breathing the breath of life into him. Later, God made woman from a rib taken from the man's side. Contrary to the evolutionary view of origins, the biblical view of people identifies them as unique from animals, created in the image and likeness of God.

The biblical view of people recognizes the existence of both a physical and metaphysical aspect of their being. The material part of a person is described as the body. The Bible teaches that people have a created body (Gen. 2:7), a physical body (1 Cor. 15:38-40), a body of death (Rom. 7:24), a body of sin (Rom. 5:19), a body of humiliation (Phil. 3:21), and a body which needs discipline (1 Cor. 6:19).

In addition to the material part of people, there is also an immaterial part most often described as the soul or spirit.

The Bible uses the term soul to identify something other than a person's physical body that cannot be defined materially (Isa. 10:18). Sometimes this term is also used to describe the whole person (Song 1:7) or the life of a person (Gen. 35:18). The term spirit is used to describe the mind (Gen. 8:1) or breath (1 Thess. 2:8). These two terms are similar and are sometimes used interchangably because they both appear to refer to the life-principle (Gen. 41:8; Ps. 42:6; John 12:27; 13:21). Yet at the same time, the Bible describes subtle differences between the soul and spirit (Heb. 4:12).

What we believe about people is based on the biblical account of the early history of humanity. The Bible teaches that God created people in His own image and likeness. One of the key words in Scripture to understand human personality is the term "heart." But the heart of people today is not the same as it was in the beginning. The failure of the ancestral parents of the human race introduced sin into human experience. Part of our understanding of people today necessarily involves understanding the nature of sin.

Made in the Image and Likeness of God

One of the things that makes people unique in God's creation is their creation in His image and likeness. These words "image and likeness" describe two aspects of our original nature which help us understand ourselves today.

The word "image" is used in both the Old and New Testament in a variety of ways. People are described as "the image of God" (1 Cor. 11:7) and "the image of Christ" (Rom. 8:20). Christ is also described as being in "the image of God" (2 Cor. 4:4). The word image is also used to describe idols (Rom. 1:23) and the imprint of a Caesar on a coin (Matt. 22:20). The use of this word suggests an image is something that is similar, with the same properties, but not necessarily identical.

When God made people in His own image, He made them similar to Himself. This means He reproduced some aspect of Himself in people. This probably had nothing to do with physical appearance since God is Spirit and not limited to a physical body. Rather, the image of God in people probably refers to their ability to think and make decisions, feel emotion, and act freely. Although the image of God in people has been marred by sin, people still retain a limited use of these faculties.

The word likeness describes the original state of innocence into which people were created. Originally, people were holy like God in the sense they had no sin nature and did not practice sin. At the Fall, this likeness was lost. Part of the saving work of Christ in our life is to restore that likeness in our life. We regain our spiritual likeness with God at conversion (Rom. 5:19). We realize a character likeness with God through sanctification (Rom. 8:29). We will experience a physical likeness with God at our glorification (1 Cor. 15:52-53; 1 John 3:2).

The Heart (Personality) of People

Another expression Scripture uses to describe people is the term "heart." This term is used to describe the personality of people. Expressions of personality such as intellect, emotions, and will are all described in the context of the heart. Also, the Bible describes the heart as the center of a person's moral awareness, the conscience. Obviously, when the Bible uses the word heart, it is talking about human personality rather than the organ which pumps blood through our bodies.

Several intellectual activities of the heart are specifically mentioned in Scripture. People think with their heart (Phil. 4:8). Planning is also described as a function of the heart (Prov. 16:9). People can hide the Word of God in their heart through Scripture memory (Ps. 119:11). Perception is also described as a function of the heart (Matt. 13:14). Finally, the ability to weigh evidence and make a rational and reasonable decision is described as an intellectual function of the heart (Mark 2:8).

Most people today would agree with the Bible's description of the heart as the emotional center of our personality. Our culture even today commonly ascribes such emotions as love and empathy as springing from one's heart. The Bible identifies several emotions springing from the heart including love (Matt. 22:37), confidence (John 14:1), joy (John 16:6), peace (Phil. 4:7), unity and gladness (Acts 2:46), hate (Matt. 15:19), fear (John 14:27), sorrow (John 16:16), frustration (Ps. 131), and division and strife (1 Cor. 1:10; 3:3).

People also exercise their will as an expression of their heart. This is especially seen in several areas. First, people are converted when they respond to the Gospel with their heart (Rom. 6:17; 10:9). Second, ongoing spiritual growth in our life also grows out of a heart response to the things of God (2 Cor. 9:7). Third, we relate to one another as Christians out of a willingness to do God's will from our heart (Eph. 6:5, 6).

Finally, the heart is also described as the seat of our moral awareness. Deep within every person is a natural consciousness of God and sense of absolute moral standards based on the character of God. The Bible describes this as a work of Christ, the Light which enlightens us (John 1:9). It is also described in Scripture as both the law of God inscribed on our heart (Rom. 2:15) and an awareness of eternal values which exists within the heart (Eccl. 3:11). While God's input into our conscience makes it a reliable guide in decision making, the conscience can also be so corrupted by sin in our life that it is virtually rendered inoperative (1 Tim. 4:2). It is important to train our conscience by the Word of God.

What Went Wrong?

As we look at what the Bible teaches about people, we find ourselves describing two kinds of people: the kind of people God made, fantastic creatures, the climax of His entire creation; and the kind of people we are today, evil in nature and corrupt in behavior. Yet these are not actually two kinds of people at all, but the same race of people at two different points in their experience.

When we look at how we began as a race and compare it to what we are today, we are bound to ask the question, "What went wrong?"

The answer to that question is found in the biblical account of the introduction of sin into the human race. When God completed His creative work, He noted all He had made was "very good" (Gen. 1:31). But when Satan entered the garden and successfully tempted our first parents to violate God's express command not to eat a certain fruit, sin became a part of the human experience, corrupting all God made. The entire race fell into sin when Adam deliberately chose by an act of his own will to disobey God and fulfill his own desires (1 Tim. 2:14).

The same Satan who caused the human race to plunge into sin is still active today directly and indirectly tempting people to do wrong. The Bible records that first sin with these words, "So when the woman saw that the tree was good for food, that it was pleasant to the eyes, and a tree desirable to make one wise, she took of the fruit and ate. She also gave to her husband with her, and he ate" (Gen. 3:6). Today, people are still tempted in these three areas, "the lust of the flesh, the lust of the eyes, and the pride of life" (1 John 2:16). Although Adam and Eve failed when tempted in these areas, Jesus was tempted in the same way and was able to overcome the Devil (Matt. 4:1-11).

By looking at the temptation of Christ, we can understand how to overcome temptation in our life today. First, each time Jesus was tempted, He responded by referring to the Word of God (Matt. 4:4, 7, 10). The Scriptures can also help us overcome temptation and prevent us from falling into sin (Ps. 119:9-11). Second, Jesus faced temptation in the fulness of the Holy Spirit (Matt. 4:1). When we walk in the Spirit, we will not fall into sin when we are tempted (Gal. 5:16).

A third key to overcoming temptation in the Christian life is to fight temptation with a winner. When you became a Christian, you received a new nature as Christ came to live within you. But you also have an old nature which you inherited from Adam. When you are tempted, you can resist in your own strength depending upon the old nature which has a losing record against sin or you can resist temptation in the power of the new nature by letting Christ who has an undefeated record against sin live His life through you.

The Nature of Sin

Sin has been described as that which is opposed to the character and will of God. Sin is something which has permeated our entire being so that it is virtually impossible to understand who we are without knowing about sin. People sin both in action and attitude.

The apostle Paul described three basic kinds of sin in his epistles. To understand how sin makes us the kind of people we are, it is important to understand each of these three kinds of sin.

The first kind of sin described in Scripture is personal sin. Comparing Jews and Gentiles, Paul concluded, "For there is no difference: for all have sinned, and come short of the glory of God" (Rom. 3:22-23). A personal sin may be a sin of commission (doing something wrong) or a sin of omission (failing to do something right). Personal sin may be expressed as an act or attitude. Sinful acts are produced by people with sinful attitudes (Mark 7:21). That is why Jesus equated sins like anger with murder (Matt. 5:21-22) and lust with fornication (Matt. 5:27-28).

When we practice personal sin, our fellowship with God is broken (Ps. 66:18). That broken fellowship can be restored as we confess our sins and accept God's forgiveness (1 John 1:9). If a person is not a Christian, he or she will not experience fellowship with God until he or she places saving faith in Jesus (Eph. 1:7).

Scripture uses various descriptions of personal sin. These include falling short (Rom. 3:23), going astray (Isa. 53:6), transgression (Ps. 51:1), and trespass (Eph. 2:1).

The second kind of sin described in Scripture is our sin nature. The word sin occurs in both the singular and plural in the Bible. Usually, when the word occurs as a singular noun, it is referring to the sin nature of people. We all have a sin nature that has been a part of us since the moment we were conceived (Ps. 51:5). The apostle John noted, "If we say that we have no sin (nature), we deceive ourselves, and the truth is not in us" (1 John 1:8).

The Bible describes sin as having a negative influence on our intellect (Rom. 1:28) and conscience (1 Tim. 4:2), two aspects of our personality. Therefore our sin nature negatively impacts our personality. Our sin nature influences us to sin (Rom. 5:12). But our sin nature has already been judged on the Cross (Rom. 6:6). While we still have the old nature, we cannot use it as an excuse for sinning because it has been crucified with Christ (Rom. 6:7).

The third way sin is described in Scripture is imputed sin. The word impute means "to ascribe to" or "reckon over." "As by one man sin entered into the world, and death by sin; and so death passed upon all men, for that all have sinned" (Rom. 5:12). When we make a purchase with a credit card, the value of that purchase is "imputed" to our account. In the same way, the sin of Adam is imputed to the human race which sprang from heaven. This is done because Adam was both the seminal and representative head of the human race. Just as a child partakes in the consequences of the wise or unwise financial investments of a father, so we live with the consequence of the imputed sin of our father Adam. Also, just as the citizens live with the consequences of decisions made by their representatives in government, so we live with the consequences of our representative's decision in the Garden of Eden.

Some might view the imputation of Adam's sin to the human race as somehow unfair or unjustified, but our willingness to so readily engage in sin like Adam suggests we would have done the same thing. Still, God not only imputes Adam's sin to the human race, but He also offers to impute Christ's righteousness to all who believe (Rom. 5:21). The biblical remedy for imputed sin is the imputed righteousness of Christ.

God created people as the high point of His creation. Although sin has marred that creation, God still loves people and wants what is best for them. The greatest evidence of God's love for these created beings is seen in what He has done to save them from the sin that threatens to destroy them. Christians who love people like God loves people will want to do their best to help them experience the salvation God has provided for their sin.

Chapter Five Review & Discussion

Review Questions

1. How were people created?

2. What are the two aspects of a person's being?

3. What does "heart" mean in the Bible?

4. What are the three kinds of sin mentioned in Scripture?

Discussion Questions

1. How can you overcome temptation?

2. What happens when a Christian sins?

3. Adam's sin was imputed to the human race, therefore we are all sinners. Have you accepted the biblical remedy – the imputed righteousness of Christ – for your sin?

Chapter Six

CHAPTER SIX

What We Believe about Salvation

The single most significant experience in life is receiving the salvation provided by Christ on the Cross. This experience is so significant that the Bible uses over a hundred different expressions to describe it. The experience is difficult to describe fully if a person has not personally experienced salvation.

The Bible uses the word *salvation* in three different ways. First, salvation is described in a past tense. In this sense we have been saved from the guilt and penalty of sin. Second, salvation is described in a present tense. This means we are being saved from the habit and dominion of sin. Third, salvation is described in a future tense. Someday, we will be saved from all the physical infirmities which are the consequence of sin and the curse of God upon sin.

The Bible uses many different expressions to describe the change that takes place in a person's life in salvation. Each expression describes the same thing from a slightly different perspective, emphasizing a particular aspect of this experience. As we examine what we believe about salvation, we will focus our study on four of these words: conversion, regeneration, justification, and sanctification.

Conversion

Bible teachers often use the word *conversion* when describing the salvation experience from a human perspective. Conversion refers to the personality change that takes place when a person becomes a Christian. This change embraces the total person, intellect, emotions, and will. The apostle Paul described the conversion experience when he wrote, "ye have obeyed from the heart that form of doctrine which was delivered you" (Rom. 6:17).

Conversion often begins with a change in thinking or acquiring new knowledge. To be converted, a person must know the Gospel. Although there is only one Gospel (Gal. 1:9), it may be described as both personal truth and propositional truth. The Gospel is personal truth because it is the person of Jesus (1 Cor. 2:2). The Gospel is also propositional truth which means it is an accurate formula because it is the death, burial, and resurrection of Christ (1 Cor. 15:1-4).

There are several things people must know to be converted. First, they must know their need, "all have sinned" (Rom. 3:23). The Bible emphasizes our need for conversion by reminding us that no one is righteous before God and all are sinners. Second, people need to know the penalty for their sin. The Bible says, "The wages of sin is death" (Rom. 6:23). This refers to both physical death (James 2:26) and the second death which is eternal separation from God (Rev. 20:14). Third, people need to know God's provision for salvation. This provision is found in the substitutionary death of Christ for our sins. Christ died for us (Rom. 5:8). As a result, God is able to offer salvation as a free gift to all who respond ("Believe in thine heart," Rom. 10:9) and receive Christ Jesus as Lord (Rom. 6:23).

THINGS PEOPLE MUST KNOW TO BE CONVERTED
Their need **The penalty for their sin** **God's provision for salvation** **How to respond to the Gospel**

Knowing the Gospel (intellectually) is foundational to the conversion experience, but just knowing is not enough. People are not converted until they apply these truths and receive Jesus (John 1:12). People need to know these truths, but they also need to know how to respond to the Gospel.

Because conversion impacts the total personality of a person, it is not surprising that emotions (feelings) are also affected in conversion. Sometimes, God will use our emotions to bring us to personal repentance and saving faith (2 Cor. 7:9-10). In the experience of others, the emotions are impacted after the conversion experience takes place (Acts 8:8). Everybody has a different way of expressing their emotions depending upon their age, sex, cultural background, and other unique experiences which have made them who they are. Therefore, everybody will have different emotional responses when they are converted. The emotional response is not that which effects conversion, but when conversion takes place one's emotions will be involved to some degree.

Ultimately, conversion involves a definite act of the will. The Bible describes people being converted with expressions like "trusting in" (Prov. 3:4), "repenting" (Acts 2:38), "believing" (Acts 16:31), "receiving" (John 1:12), "being born again" (John 3:7), "calling" and "confessing" (Rom. 10:9). Each of these verbs implies involving one's will in the conversion experience.

People are converted when they repent of their sin and believe the Gospel. When Jesus preached, He said, "Repent ye, and believe in the Gospel" (Mark 1:15). Repentance means to turn around, change your mind about sin in such a way that it results in a change of action. Saving faith takes place when a person trusts God for salvation depending upon the finished work of Christ on the Cross. In the conversion experience, repentance and saving faith are two sides of the same coin. When people are converted, they turn from their sins (repentance) to faith in God (1 Thess. 1:9-10). Biblical repentance and saving faith do not exist apart from each other.

Conversion may be viewed as both a process and an event. Many Christians vividly remember the exact context in which they were converted. Others can remember a time prior to their conversion and know they are now converted, but have difficulty identifying the exact "hour of decision." In both cases, their conversion experience was part of a much larger conversion process.

Some Christians object to viewing conversion as a process fearing it may lead to the conclusion that a person can earn salvation or can become a Christian without being converted. Both conclusions are wrong. Salvation is a gift from God (Eph. 2:8-9). Also, Jesus expressly told Nicodemus, "Unless one is born again, he cannot see the kingdom of God" (John 3:3).

Regeneration

Regeneration is the work of God through the Holy Spirit within a person who has "saving faith," in which a new nature is given that makes the person capable of doing the will of God. Whereas conversion looks at the salvation experience from a human perspective, regeneration describes the same experience from a divine perspective. While the term regeneration occurs in only one verse to describe this experience (Tit. 3:5), it is also described as being "born again" (John 3:3, 7).

The Bible teaches several things about being born again. First, this is an act of God. Only God can forgive sin and save a soul (Mark 2:7). Second, regeneration produces spiritual life in the believer. Paul described the Ephesian Christians as "dead in trespasses and sins" prior to their being made alive in Christ (Eph. 2:1). This new life given Christians when they believe in Christ as Saviour has been described as *The Life of God in the Soul of Man.* When a person is born again, both the Father and Son (John 14:23) and the Holy Spirit (Rom. 8:11) take up residence in the believer. The new life in the Christian is Christ living in and through him or her (Gal. 2:20).

Because the new life in regeneration is tied to the indwelling presence of God in the believer, regeneration understandably produces noticeable changes. Perhaps the first of these noticeable changes is a new nature. This new nature is inclined to serve God and enables the believer to control the old sinful nature and live a victorious Christian life. Second, the Christian is transformed into a new creation (2 Cor. 5:17). This change was extremely dramatic in the experience of many Corinthian believers. Those who had been unfaithful, idol worshipers, homosexuals, thieves, alcoholics, terrorists, and extortioners were transformed into Christian believers by the Spirit of God (1 Cor. 6:9-11). For others, the change may be less dramatic but just as real.

The basis of both conversion and regeneration is the Scriptures which are the instrument of salvation and the Holy Spirit who is the agent of salvation. The Bible convicts of sin (John 16:9-11), gives us a new nature (2 Peter 1:4), and is the basis of our spiritual power to overcome sin (Ps. 119:9-11). It effects a new birth in our life (1 Peter 1:23). The Holy Spirit is the agent of salvation – the Person who convicts of sin, draws people to Christ, and gives new life to those who repent. When we come to saving faith in Christ, we are indwelt by the Holy Spirit and "the Spirit Himself bears witness with our spirit that we are children of God" (Rom. 8:15).

Justification

While there are many things which happen in the experience of the Christian at the moment of salvation, there are also a number of things which happen outside the realm of experience which are nevertheless just as real. The conversion/regeneration experience coincides with a legal declaration of our righteous standing before God. This aspect of salvation is called "justification." This exciting aspect of the doctrine of salvation gave birth to the Protestant Reformation.

Justification is the act whereby God declares a person righteous when he or she trusts Christ. It is the means by which God establishes a legal relationship between God and people. It doesn't make people perfect but rather declares them perfect in God's sight. Someone has put it this way: "Justification means God sees me 'just-as-if' I'd never sinned!"

Justification is non-experiential. It gives us a new standing before God and is the means by which we enter into a new position in the heavenlies (Eph. 2:6). It is a judicial act on the part of God that results in our having peace with God (Rom. 5:1). The Bible describes justification in several contexts. The possibility of our justification was accomplished by the atoning death of Christ (Rom. 3:24-25). Justification is applied to the life of the Christian when he or she exercises justifying faith (Rom. 5:1). We give evidence of the reality of our justification by the good works which issue from our life (James 2:18, 24).

Abraham is the first person in Scripture who is described as having been justified by faith (Gen. 15:6). Abraham did not consider the circumstances of his life which made the realization of God's promise to him seem impossible, but was "fully persuaded that, what he (God) had promised, he was able also to perform" (Rom. 4:21). This faith in God resulted in his justification (Gen. 15:6). Later, Abraham demonstrated the reality of his faith by doing what God wanted Him to do (James 2:21).

Some people fail to understand the relationship between faith and works in justification. They attempt to impress God with a variety of good works hoping to be accepted by God. But the Bible teaches that our sin has separated us from God. Even if we were to live perfect lives from this day until the day we die, the sins we have already committed would stand in the way of our being declared righteous. The only way we can be justified before God is to accept Christ's righteousness by faith. Then when His righteousness has become our righteousness, we will naturally want to do the kind of good works He did, demonstrating to others the change which has already taken place in our life.

In justification, God declares us not guilty of sin and we have a perfect record in heaven. When He looks at us, He sees the record of His Son and applies it to our case.

Justification is the act whereby our legal position in heaven is changed. This act in and of itself does not change the person being justified. But as that person begins to realize what was involved in his or her justification, it will be expressed in a new lifestyle. When a person is declared a citizen of a new country, there is no physical change in the person. But as he or she begins to apply the benefits of citizenship, that person begins to do things that would not have been allowed or done previously (voting, enjoying certain liberties, etc.).

We are justified at our conversion. It often takes time to experience the change which has taken place in our life. The process by which we apply our salvation to a lifestyle which becomes more Christlike is called "sanctification."

The key to sanctification is letting Christ live His life fully through our life (Gal. 2:20). The apostle Paul describes this process throughout his epistles, but perhaps never so clearly as in Romans 6. In that chapter, he used four verbs to describe the practical steps in working out our personal salvation into a consistent Christian lifestyle.

The first of these four verbs is "know" (Rom. 6:3, 6, 9). Our actions as Christians are the result of certain attitudes which are based on biblical truth. Paul wanted us to know that we have been identified with Christ in His death. This means that just as Christ had victory over death, so we also can have victory over the old nature which has been crucified with Christ. Knowing we can have spiritual victory is the first step in experiencing that victory.

The second word used by Paul is "reckon" (Rom. 6:11). This word means to count on or rely upon this to be true. If we know the old nature is "dead," we should count on this to be true when we face temptation. If that part of our life is dead, we should not try to revive it by encouraging it to sin. Rather, reckon it dead and don't sin.

The third key verb in this chapter is "yield" (Rom. 6:13). It is not enough to simply not respond to sin with the old nature. We also need to respond positively to God with our new nature. Yielding to God means that we give Him the "right of way" in our life.

Finally, Paul also used the word "obey" (Rom. 6:16-17) to describe the fourth step in this process. Obedience is the natural implication of recognizing Jesus as Lord in our life. Regardless of what we say, the one we are most ready to obey is the real Lord in our life. When we fail to obey Christ, we deny His lordship in that area of our life.

The process of sanctification is similar to a child learning to walk. As the child takes his or her first steps, that child begins walking. But usually the new walker will stumble and fall many times before walking becomes second nature. This is often the experience in the Christian life as we attempt to "walk worthy of the vocation wherewith ye are called" (Eph. 4:1). As you begin taking these steps, there may be times when you stumble and fall. This does not mean you will never be successful in living the Christian life, only that you are learning. Like the child who stumbles, you need to get up again and try taking another step. At first, you may have to concentrate on each step and strive to keep balance in your Christian life. But as you become more experienced in your Christian life, you will find these steps in your walk becoming a second nature.

Chapter Six Review & Discussion

Review Questions

1. What is conversion?

2. What is the basis of conversion and regeneration?

3. What is justification/how are we justified?

Discussion Questions

1. How can you be sanctified?

2. What are the steps to having a consistent Christian lifestyle?

3. What should you do if you "stumble and fall" in your Christian life?

Chapter Seven

Chapter Seven

CHAPTER SEVEN
What We Believe about the Church

Different people have different ideas about the meaning of the word "church." Sometimes people use the term to describe a building in the community decorated with religious symbols. Others describe the church as a social group to which they belong. Still others use the term to describe a particular denomination such as the Church of England or the Roman Catholic Church. And there are others who use this term as an expression to describe the entity to which all Christians belong (the universal church).

Outside the Christian community, people have other ideas about the church. For some, it is a community group which sponsors a particular service they find helpful such as a day-care center. Others see the church as the place they meet others like themselves in a ladies' coffee hour or a support group. Some think of it as a place to send their children on Sunday morning so they can sleep in. Others see it as a somewhat irrelevant institution which may have had its place in a previous generation.

Jesus knew we would need help living the Christian life, so He promised, "I will build my church" (Matt. 16:18). He provided the church as a means of Christians assembling together to encourage and help one another in the Christian life. This would enable church members to be more effective in reaching out to others in their community. Because the church has such a prominent role in the plan of God for His people, it is important for us to understand what makes a church a church, what a church is supposed to do, what is involved in church membership, and how we should respond to church leadership. While each church and denomination has its particular distinctives, it is important to understand the biblical answer to these four important questions.

What Makes a Church a Church?

The Greek word *ekklesia,* translated "church" in the New Testament, was widely used in the first century to describe a group that was called out from the larger community for a specific purpose. In this general way, the word is used to describe a trade guild (Acts 19:32, 39, 41), a general gathering as in Israel in the wilderness (Acts 7:38), and a synagogue meeting (Matt. 18:17). But the word is also used in a more technical way to describe the gathering of the early Christians.

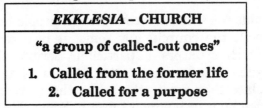

***EKKLESIA* – CHURCH**
"a group of called-out ones"
1. Called from the former life   **2. Called for a purpose**

A local church is more than just a gathering of Christians. It must assemble for the right purpose, have the right authority, reproduce itself, have the right organization, and have the seal of God on its existence. A church may be described as an assembly of professing believers in whom Christ dwells, organized to carry out the Great Commission, administer the ordinances, and reflect spiritual gifts under the discipline of the Scriptures.

A local church needs to be organized to accomplish its function. The nature of church life is described in the experience of the church at Jerusalem (Acts 2:41-47). These functions can be described using the acrostic WIFE which stands for Worship, Instruction, Fellowship, and Evangelism. An easy way to remember this is to recall that one of the biblical pictures of a church is that of a bride. Every bride wants to be a good wife, therefore, every church should be organized to accomplish these functions.

THE FUNCTION OF A CHURCH
Worship
Instruction
Fellowship
Evangelism

The early church was a worshipping church, constantly engaged in "praising God" (Acts 2:47). Many evangelical churches today describe their Sunday morning service as a "worship service." When we worship God, we seek to serve Him with our praises thus inviting Him into our midst in a unique way (Ps. 22:3). Worship also helps us by meeting our needs with God's sufficiency.

The early church was involved in instructing people in the apostle's doctrine (Acts 2:42). Today, churches organize to accomplish this function through a Christian education board or discipleship training ministry. Such organizations help insure the church's success in instructing its members.

Fellowship was the third significant activity of the early church (Acts 2:42, 44). God has recognized from the very beginning that people need people (Gen. 2:18). One of the unique functions of the church is to provide opportunity for Christians to interact with one another informally as a means of motivating one another in their Christian life (Heb. 10:25).

Evangelism was the fourth function of the early church. This church began with an evangelistic thrust in which three thousand people were saved (Acts 2:41). Evangelism continued to be an integral part of church life resulting in others being converted to Christianity daily (Acts 2:47). Before long, their aggressive witness for Christ "filled Jerusalem" (Acts 5:28) and turned their world upside down (Acts 17:6). They believed in using every available means to reach every available person at every available time with the Gospel.

Obviously, not all of these functions can be accomplished in the same way. In the New Testament, the church met in smaller cells to accomplish ministry (Acts 12:12) and larger gatherings for celebration (Acts 3:11). This pattern has been followed throughout church history by growing churches. Today, many churches gather in a large worship service for celebration, but also gather in smaller Bible study groups such as Sunday School classes, home Bible study cells or specialized ministry teams for personal growth and ministry.

What Is the Purpose of the Church?

Every institution can only justify its existence as it accomplishes the purpose for which it was established. The church's purpose is found in the Great Commission (Matt. 28:19-20). Often, the Great Commission is applied to foreign missions but neglected at home. Actually, the task of making disciples needs to be accomplished both at home by involved church members and abroad through the missionary outreach of the church.

At the heart of the Great Commission is the task of making disciples (Matt. 28:19). Therefore, evangelism is more than decision-making, it is disciple-making. Evangelism may be described as communicating the Gospel in the power of the Holy Spirit to unconverted persons at their point of need, with the intent of effecting conversions and involving them in the church. Some people consider any Christian presence in society as an expression of evangelism. Others define evangelism in the context of preaching the Gospel. While both of these are important, they are only steps in the process of persuading people to put their faith in Christ as Saviour and follow Him as Lord in the fellowship of His church.

Jesus described three steps which are necessary if the church is to be successful in fulfilling her mission. First, the church must take the Gospel to the people (Matt. 28:19). The goal of this step is to bring people to the point of making a personal decision for salvation. The next step is described by the verb "baptizing" (Matt. 28:19), which involves assimilating the new believer into the life of the church. The task of baptism results in bonding or identification. Third, the task of teaching results in new believers being trained in the Christian life and witness (Matt. 28:20).

What Does Church Membership Involve?

The doctrine of the church is not some abstract teaching which has little or no relevance to the Christian life. Rather, the church ought to have a central place in the life of every believer. Often, people come to faith in Christ through a church-related ministry. As the new believer struggles to grow in his or her new life in Christ, church ministries and individual church members play a key role in helping him or her experience success. The church is where we find ministry opportunities that enable us to use our spiritual gifts to touch other lives.

Church membership is an expression of belonging. When people join a church, they are telling others they feel at home in that church and want to be a full participant in the life of the church. Therefore, church membership involves more than just adding your name to the role. It is an expression of your desire to be enfolded into the church family. It provides you with the opportunity to be involved in the lives of others.

For many, church membership has lost its meaning.
The Bible teaches that every Christian is "baptized into
one body" (1 Cor. 12:13). This refers to the baptism of
the Holy Spirit by which all Christians are one in
Christ. But the Bible also uses the expression "body of
Christ" to describe the local church (1 Cor. 12:27).
Therefore, when Christians are baptized and join a
church, they demonstrate outwardly what has already
happened inwardly. Because they become a part of the
body of Christ by receiving Him as Saviour (John 1:12),
they want to become an active member of a local church
which is a local expression of the body of Christ.

When a Christian moves into a new community and
begins to worship at a new church, it is only natural for
him or her to want to change church membership. Just
as people change their address and phone number when
they move, so they should also change their church
membership (their spiritual home) when they move.

Some Christians have not yet taken the very natural step to become a member of the church. When Paul
described the church as a body, he reminded us that
each of us is an important part of that body. We use
terms such as handicapped, disabled and disadvantaged
to describe a physical body which is missing an eye, ear,
arm or foot. These terms could also be applied to many
churches which are lacking parts because of the reluctance of some Christians to become involved.

Joining a church places us under the discipline of
the Scriptures – the Word of God. God gave us the Bible
to help us grow spiritually (1 Peter 2:2), achieve victory
over sin (Ps. 119:9-11), see our prayers answered (John
15:7), develop strong character (1 Cor. 3:3), and grow in
our ability to believe God (Rom. 10:17). As we hear the
Word of God preached and study the Scriptures with
others in small groups, we can begin to experience these
benefits in our own life.

God made us to need relationships with others. Becoming a part of a church provides us with the opportunity to encourage others and be encouraged by others (Heb. 10:25). In the New Testament, those who received Christ as Saviour quickly chose to become part of the church (Acts 2:41). As they interacted with each other on a regular basis, they were able to build a steadfastness into their life in various spiritual disciplines (Acts 2:42). Becoming active in the life of a church is one way of insuring personal success in your Christian life.

Evangelical Christians look to the New Testament to determine what is involved in joining a church. In the New Testament, church membership was related to four conditions. First, no one joined a church until they had first received Christ as personal Saviour (Acts 5:13-14). Second, Christians were baptized as a profession of their faith prior to joining a church (Acts 2:41). Third, Christians remained members of a church only as long as they remained in agreement with the church's doctrinal beliefs (Titus 3:10). Fourth, church members were responsible to live moral lives so as to not hinder the corporate testimony of the church (1 Cor. 6:9-11).

Just as the parts of your physical body work together in harmony to enable you to do things, so church members need to work together to enable the church to accomplish its ministry. There are several ways church members can invest in their local church. They can make a special effort to give time to church services and ministry projects (Eph. 5:16). They can use their spiritual gifts as ministry tools in the church (Eph. 4:12). They can consistently give to the church to underwrite the costs associated with the church's ministry (1 Cor. 16:2). They can help build others in the church (Heb. 10:25). They can use their influence to help others receive Christ as Saviour and become a part of church life.

Joining a church is more than adding your name to the membership list. By joining a church, you indicate your desire to be involved in the life of the church, and to have others in the church involved in your life. You become part of a family. As such, you are entitled to all the privileges associated with family life and assume the responsibility of making that family work.

How Do I Respond to Church Leadership?

Obviously, whenever a group of people meet together, there must be an efficient organizational structure to insure that group accomplishes its purpose. This involves appointing a leader and often selecting others who have lesser leadership responsibilities in the group. The need for group leadership exists in the church just as it exists in other groups.

The leader of the church is the Lord Jesus Christ Himself. He is described as "the head of the body, the church" and the One who alone holds preeminence in the church (Col. 1:18). The Bible records the case of one church leader named Diotrephes and is critical of his desire "to have the preeminence among them" (3 John 9). That position belongs to Christ alone.

While Christ is the leader of the church, He has appointed pastors to provide leadership in the church through the pastoral office. Paul reminded the Ephesian elders of their pastoral responsibilities "to all the flock, over which the Holy Ghost hath made you overseers" (Acts 20:28). Likewise Peter encouraged pastors to willingly be overseers of the church for the right motives (1 Peter 5:2). Pastors have this important responsibility because God holds them accountable for the spiritual well being of those under their leadership (Heb. 13:17). As church members, it is our responsibility to pray for, support, and follow our pastors as they lead.

Pastors are not the only officers in the church. God also established the office of deacons in the church. The word *deacon* could be translated *servant* which better describes the nature of this office. The first deacons were selected by the church and appointed by the apostles to do ministry and restore harmony in the church (Acts 6:1-6). As a result of their faithful ministry, "the word of God spread, and the number of the disciples multiplied greatly in Jerusalem, and a great many of the priests were obedient to the faith" (Acts 6:7).

Most evangelical churches are congregational in government. This means that the church congregation itself is the final authority in major decisions such as the calling of a pastor, the purchase or sale of property, and the approval of the church budget. This congregational approach to church government is the same as democracy. However, the church is a theocracy under the Lordship of Christ. When Christians meet to make church decisions, they should vote on the basis of what they believe the Lord would like to see happen in His church, not on the basis of what they would like.

Jesus promised He would build His church (Matt. 16:18). When we become fully involved in the life of the church, we are working with Christ in doing what He is doing (1 Cor. 3:9). That opportunity alone should motivate us to become as fully involved as possible in the ministry of a local Bible-believing church in our community.

Chapter Seven Review & Discussion

Review Questions

1. What is a church?

2. What acrostic describes four functions of the church and what are those functions?

3. What is the purpose of the church?

Discussion Questions

1. What does membership in your church involve?

2. How do you respond to church leadership?

3. When a decision needs to be made within the church and a vote is taken, what do you base your decision on?

Chapter Eight

CHAPTER EIGHT

What We Believe about Eschatology

The word "eschatology" literally means "the study of last things." Therefore, it is fitting that this last study in what we believe should deal with what we believe about eschatology. Our "last study" in Christian doctrine will focus on "last things."

The doctrine of eschatology is really two doctrines unified by a chronological theme. Sometimes, when Christians talk about eschatology, they talk about personal eschatology. Personal eschatology is the study of God's final judgments and the eternal state, heaven and hell. At other times, Christians use the term eschatology to describe Bible prophecy. Prophetic eschatology is the study of the second coming of Christ and the various events related to His return (the signs of His coming, the Rapture, Great Tribulation, and the kingdom).

Some Christians seek to minimize the study of eschatology. They see the many abuses of this doctrine by those who have strayed from the truth of Scripture and are concerned that others do not do the same. These abuses include date-setting, making controversy over minor points, ignoring the future, getting caught up in details and forgetting Christ. Other people recall controversy in a church over some relatively minor prophetic teaching and equate the study of Bible prophecy with divisiveness. But about forty percent of the Bible was prophetic when it was written, therefore, the student of the Bible must study prophecy or neglect a vast part of the Scriptures. It is important to avoid the abuses of this doctrine. This can best be accomplished by an understanding of what the Bible teaches.

As is the case with other doctrines, some Christians have minor differences of opinion concerning some of the more exact details of the interpretation of prophecy. But there are two areas in which all evangelical Christians agree concerning the return of Christ. The first is the certainty that He will in fact return. This is the basis for our hope as Christians. The second is that He may return at any moment, perhaps before you complete reading this chapter. This is the basis for our motivation in Christian service.

When we study Bible prophecy, we should not study the Scriptures exclusively to learn details and arrange prophetic charts. A correct understanding of prophetic truth will impact the way we live our lives.

First, prophetic truth motivates us to develop Christian character. Prophetic truth is taught in Scripture as an incentive to godliness (Titus 2:12-13), holiness (2 Peter 3:11), joyfulness (1 Peter 1:8), patience (James 5:8), purity (1 John 3:3), faith (John 14:1-3), sobriety (1 Peter 1:13), moderation (Phil. 4:5), sincerity (Phil. 1:9-11), faithfulness (Rev. 2:25; 3:11), discernment (1 Cor. 4:5), accountability (Matt. 25:19), and righteousness (Titus 2:12).

Second, prophetic truth motivates us in our Christian life. Prophetic truth is taught in Scripture as an incentive to obedience (1 Tim. 6:13-14), repentance (Rev. 3:3), watchfulness (1 Thess. 5:6), abiding in Christ (1 John 2:28), brotherly love (1 Thess. 3:12), discipleship (Luke 9:26), readiness (1 Peter 1:13), mortification of the flesh (Col. 3:4-5), personal separation (1 Thess. 5:22-23), bearing persecution (1 Peter 4:13), enduring the trial of faith (1 Peter 1:7), every good work (2 Thess. 2:12), and faithful church attendance (Heb. 10:35).

Third, prophetic truth also motivates us to become involved in Christian service. This truth is described in Scripture as an incentive to preaching (2 Thess. 4:1–2), shepherding (1 Peter 5:2-4), comforting one another (1 Thess. 4:18), teaching (Matt. 28:20), and evangelism (1 Thess. 2:19-20).

Signs of the Times

Over the years, scientists have noticed a cause and effect relationship between certain activities. A certain kind of cloud always appears in the sky prior to a thunderstorm. Birds consistently begin flying in formation just prior to their annual migrations. Fish swim up rivers just before spawning. Trees blossom before bearing fruit. Since God established His world in such a predictable pattern, it should not be surprising that He has also established certain signs to indicate the second coming of Christ.

Two passages of Scripture are generally interpreted by students of prophecy as prophetic accounts of the course of this age. In the kingdom parables of Matthew 13, Jesus taught the growth of Christendom as a result of sowing the Gospel, and the eventual judgment of God to discern that which is worth saving and that which cannot be salvaged. In the church epistles of Revelation 2 and 3, Jesus addressed seven churches which represent seven periods of church history. Many Bible teachers believe the apathetic Laodicean church (Rev. 3:14-22) represents the church today, indicating that the return of Christ may be very soon.

In addition to these prophetic pictures of church history, many Bible teachers also look to Israel as an indicator of the soon return of Christ. God's character demands that He honor His covenant with Abraham (Gen. 12:1-6). Scripture describes a restoration of Israel to the promised land (Ezek. 37:11-14). Some Bible teachers see the establishment of the State of Israel in 1948, the expansion of its territory during the Six Day War of 1967, and the declaration of Jerusalem as its capital during the summer of 1980 as partial fulfillments of this prophecy. But the Bible also teaches a regeneration of the nation (Ezek. 37:14). Today, Israel is in the land in unbelief (Deut. 30:1-3), but the stage may be set for a great national revival which will result in many coming to Christ (Rom. 11:25-26).

The growth of internationalism is also viewed by some as a sign of Christ's soon return. Scripture describes the presence of a world government (Rev. 13:7) and world religion (Rev. 17:1) in the final days prior to the Christ's return. With a growing number of political and free trade alliances being established around the world and a greater ecumenical spirit among nominal Christian churches and some non-Christian faith communities, it is easy to conceive of these things quickly coming into being.

The Rapture of the Church

The next event on God's prophetic time-table appears to be the rapture of the church. While there are certain signs associated with the second coming of Christ, there appears to be no pre-conditions established for the rapture of the church. Although the word "rapture" does not occur in Scripture, it is described in both 1 Corinthians 15 and 1 Thessalonians 4. The word rapture means "caught away" and is used in the Latin versions of 1 Thessalonians 4:17. That verse describes the moment when Christians who are alive when the Rapture occurs will be "caught up" to meet the Lord in the air.

Scripture appears to distinguish between the Rapture and the revelation of Christ in power and glory. In the Rapture, Christians meet Christ in the air (1 Thess. 4:13) whereas in the revelation, Christ stands on the Mount of Olives (Zech. 14:4, 9). Following the Rapture, believers are judged and rewarded (2 Cor. 5:10). The revelation is followed by judgment and condemnation of unbelievers (2 Thess. 1:7). The doctrine of the Rapture is a message of comfort (1 Thess. 4:18) but the doctrine of the revelation is a message of judgment (1 Thess. 5:4-9).

Not all Christians agree concerning the time of the Rapture in relationship to other prophetic events. Some see it as taking place during or toward the end of the Great Tribulation period, but others argue the Christian will not experience the wrath of God poured out on the world during that period (1 Thess. 5:9). Regardless of when one believes the Rapture occurs on their prophetic chart, Scripture teaches that it could occur at any moment (2 Peter 3:8-10). When we argue over when the Rapture may occur and fail to live in anticipation of it taking place imminently, we have failed to understand the biblical teaching of the Rapture.

The Great Tribulation

Much of Bible prophecy is tied to God's commitment to His people, Israel. Daniel was told that God will deal with the nation for "seventy weeks" (Dan. 9:24). Each day in that prophecy represented one year. At the end of the sixty-ninth week, the Messiah would be cut off (Dan. 9:25). This coincides historically with the crucifixion of Christ. This leaves one more week (seven years) of God's unique dealings with Israel. Most Bible teachers refer to this future seven-year period of judgment as "The Great Tribulation."

Scripture describes this period of world history as a time of great distress (Zeph. 1:15), judgment (Rev. 14:7), darkness (Amos 5:18, 20), and suffering (Matt. 24:21). In the account of this period in Revelation, three distinct series of judgments come upon the earth. The first is associated with opening a seven-sealed scroll in heaven (Rev. 6:1-17; 8:1). The second is associated with blowing seven trumpets in heaven (Rev. 8:1-10:19). The third series of judgments are portrayed as bowls of God's wrath being poured out upon the earth (Rev. 16:1-21).

Every indication in Scripture is that this future period will mark the darkest days the world has ever experienced. The world is described as being in total chaos under the leadership of a Satan-inspired political leader. There will be significant losses of life and serious negative environmental changes that make life on earth unbearable. Ultimately, the most powerful economic centers of the world will collapse with international consequences. Although this period may begin with the promise of peace, it will be marked by conflict especially directed at the nation Israel and end in an ultimate conflict with the hosts of heaven.

The Kingdom of God

At the end of this tribulation period, "the sign of the Son of Man will appear in heaven" (Matt. 24:30). Jesus will return as He promised to establish the kingdom of heaven on earth. For a thousand years, He will bring about a reign of peace on earth under conditions of general prosperity. The Old Testament prophets often looked to this kingdom age as a ray of ultimate hope for the nation of Israel which was so often subject to judgment because of their reluctance to repent of sin.

The kingdom period of world history is described as a time when creation will be released from the bondage of corruption in which it now exists (Rom. 8:21). This suggests that the environmental problems which characterize the Great Tribulation will be corrected in the Christ's return. Also, the chaos which characterizes the end of the tribulation period will also be replaced by an orderly state of affairs under the authority of Jesus, the King of Kings and Lord of Lords. Jerusalem will become His royal capital and Palestine will once again be the center of world activity. Everything about this kingdom period is described in the most desirable terms in Scripture.

The Judgments of God

At the end of the thousand years, there is one final rebellion. Satan, who had been restricted during this period, is released to lead one final attack. Some who have been born during the kingdom period but have not come to personal saving faith appear to follow Satan in this doomed attack. This period of human history – "the millineum" – ends with casting Satan and all his followers "into the lake of fire" (Rev. 20:14).

The Lake of Fire is one of several judgements described in Scripture. The Cross was God's judgment upon sin (Gal. 3:13). Believers are encouraged to engage in self-judgment (1 Cor. 11:28). God engages in a disciplinary judgment of His own much as a father who faithfully disciplines his own children (Heb. 12:3-11). After the Rapture of the church, Christians will appear before the judgment seat of Christ to receive their rewards (1 Cor. 3:12-15). God will also judge the Gentile nations on the basis of their treatment of His "brethren" (Matt. 25:32-45). In addition to the Great Tribulation and final judgment at the end of the kingdom age, the Bible also teaches that angels will be judged (1 Cor. 6:3).

Hell

When people think of the judgment of God, they usually think of hell sooner or later. Actually, most Christians prefer not to think of hell, especially if they understand something of its nature. The Bible describes hell as the eternal destiny of Satan and all those who refuse God's gracious offer of salvation.

Some people object to the Bible's teaching concerning hell, claiming a loving God would never send people to hell. The testimony of Scripture is that our loving God does everything in His power apart from violating a person's will to encourage him or her not to go to hell. Those who spend eternity in hell are those who choose not to spend it with God. The reality of hell ought to motivate us to work hard to reach people for Christ and thus depopulate hell by populating heaven.

Heaven

While some people struggle with believing in hell, few struggle with the concept of heaven. Heaven is everything we could want or wish for that is good for us. When John described heaven, he described it as the very best of the city (gold streets, brightly lit) and the very best of the country (the pure river of life, healthy trees). He described heaven not only by what he saw, but by what he saw missing (no death, sorrow, crying).

The Bible uses several expressions to describe both heaven and hell, but in both cases those expressions are probably limited. Hell is probably far worse than we could imagine with our limited human ability. In contrast, heaven is probably far greater than we could ever hope in our wildest imagination. As she closed her eyes in death, a dying saint said, "I didn't realize it would be so beautiful." Many of us may be surprised at how beautiful heaven is when we first walk through those gates.

The early church "continued steadfastly in the apostle's doctrine" (Acts 2:42). This means they had a basic understanding of biblical doctrine upon which they built stability into their Christian life. As you have engaged in this introductory study of Bible doctrine, you too have been given the opportunity to begin developing that foundation in your life. As you continue in your Christian life, you will want to learn more and reinforce your doctrinal foundation. But more than just learning doctrine, you should apply these doctrinal truths to life and

build stability into your own Christian life. The Lord
bless you in this pursuit.

Chapter Eight Review & Discussion

Review Questions

1. What is eschatology?

2. What is the Rapture?

3. What will happen during the Great Tribulation?

Discussion Questions

1. How does prophetic truth motivate you?

2. How would you describe hell? Heaven?

3. Why is it important to learn about doctrinal truths
    and know all you can about your own doctrinal posi-
    tion?

Notes

from this study
and about your church's
doctrinal beliefs

NOTES

Use this section for notes and to write an overview of your own church's doctrinal stand regarding the eight doctrines addressed in this book.

Would you like to teach this material to others?

A majority of Christians have just enough knowledge and experience to know why a person needs salvation and how to accept Christ as Saviour. They know the Gospel in a nutshell, but have never been taught the foundational doctrines of their faith. In order for Christians to remain steadfast and grow stronger in their faith, they need to know what they believe and why they believe it.

The packet was created to help you teach eight basic, foundational doctrines found in this book to your church — established members as well as new Christians.

This packet includes this textbook; a step-by-step planning agenda with convenient fold-out calendar; teaching helps with instructions, a sermon outline, and lesson handouts (with and without answers), and even brief lesson/coloring sheets for children; a promotion section with suggested announcements, sample letters, posters, and three audiocassettes of the eight lessons being taught by Dr. Elmer Towns, the author. An optional videocassette of the lessons is also available.